SCALE COLOUR FOR MODELLERS

SCALE COLOUR
FOR MODELLERS

Edited by Ian Peacock

ARGUS BOOKS

Argus Books
Argus House
Boundary Way
Hemel Hempstead
Herts HP2 7ST
England

First published by Argus Books 1991
© In this collection Argus Books 1991

ISBN 1 85486 026 7

Phototypesetting by The Works, Exeter, Devon
Printed and bound in Great Britain by Clays Ltd, St Ives plc, Bungay, Suffolk.

CONTENTS

ACKNOWLEDGEMENTS

The Publishers would like to thank the following:

Chapter 1	*Introduction*	Ian Huntley
Chapter 2	*Scale Model Colour and Metal Finish Techniques*	Ian Huntley
Chapter 3	*Metal Finishing the SnJ Way*	Peter Fearon
Chapter 4	*Painting: Hints and Tips*	Scale Models Staff
Chapter 5	*Early Aircraft — Some Guidance*	Ray Rimmel
Chapter 6	*Small-Scale Vehicles*	David Jane
Chapter 7	*AFVs — Useful Techniques*	Bob Jones
Chapter 8	*Aero Camouflage Techniques*	Ray Rimmel & Steve Archibald
Chapter 9	*Painting Model Ships*	Tony Buckley & Roger Chesneau
Chapter 10	*Custom Spraying — The Techniques Explained*	Ray Habgood
Chapter 11	*Decals — A Guide to Care and Application*	Scale Models Staff
Chapter 12	*The Fine Art of Airbrushing*	Ian Peacock
Chapter 13	*One Man's Approach to Airbrushing*	David Bailey

SCALE COLOUR FOR MODELLERS

Chapter 1

INTRODUCTION

A first rate model could only be so described because three important factors had been carefully carried out: *shape*, *texture* and *colour*.

From a scale point of view all three should be miniatures of the real thing, but as most modellers know it is not always possible to use the *actual* materials used on the full-scale subject. Therefore it is up to the skill and determination of the modeller to simulate effects whereby a polystyrene base is disguised to represent such widely differing compositions from chromed steel to linen fabric. As to the three factors and their influence, *shape* is fairly obvious in its definition. *Texture* is not always so readily recognised, but as texture is closely related to colour, it is very necessary, for example, to distinguish that a uniform coat of gloss black does not really represent a rubber tyre! So in those terms whatever time and skill was applied to achieving a true model profile and section, then at least the same amount of time should be applied to achieving the texture and colour of the model, whether ship, vehicle or aircraft.

Colour after all is in fact *the model*, for this is what the eye sees first. It is the photosphere, the visual impression, the living scene if you like, and it is the recognition of the detail by anyone closely observing a model that creates the interest. Therefore in many respects it is the more important half of modelling because a one hundred per cent accurate shape will not fully come to life unless the colour work is truly representative.

Often the trouble is that we are so used to seeing things in colour that we take it for granted and if something is green, then the tendency can be to paint it uniformly in a green thought to be somewhere near the mark. In actual fact a closer study would have revealed a specific green with certain areas dulled and faded or stained and chipped in very subtle ways, and usually in very much of a patchwork quilt effect in terms of a network or skin joints, panels or rivet lines and other surface detail.

Of course the colour problem does not really end there because as soon as the word *scale* is mentioned not only does the shape of the full-scale subject become translated into a scale shape in the model, but the colour must also become translated into scale colour. The effect can be likened to the landscape artist who puts on canvas a miniature scene of that spread in front of him in which the colours used are those he *sees at that range* and not the colours of the various subjects as would be found and measured in close-up. In other words, the colours on canvas a foot or so from the eye equal those observed some seventy feet or so away from the artist's eye, thus the colours reproduced on a three-dimensional model should equally well represent the colours seen at a distance where both model and full-scale subject are equal in size and shape.

In general it can be taken that the modification to the colour for application to a model, particularly where the model is 1/72nd scale or less, is that it should be scaled down in thickness of pigment particle size and in coating, also that it should be a tint or so lighter in hue. Both glossy and matt surfaces in full-scale should become semi-gloss on the model, although the latter should have sufficient gloss to just start to show a surface sheen. As to the tinting of the colour, a little added white or light grey will help towards this end, but it does depend on the base colour and often a spot of another stronger colour is needed to keep the colour still within its right avenue. This all goes to show that a dip out of the paint can used for the full-scale subject is only really suitable for a full-scale replica. Before making modifications to colours it is really essential to know *exactly* the colours of the full-scale subject, which is where our colour tables come in.

It is also important to know the original surface textures as well so that these can be simulated on the model and this is particularly important when it comes to model photography, for if the texture and the colour is correct then the tonal values on the film plate should be *near enough identical* to those in a photograph of the full-scale subject. So if certain colours on the model come out too darkly then it could be that there was simply not enough light, but if filmed in direct sunlight and the same has taken place, then it could be that the hue was wrong or that the model had too much of a rough surface, or even a mixture of both.

To achieve a good model too much attention to the surface texture and colouration of the full-scale subject cannot come amiss and no amount of imagination can really substitute for a prolonged study of such important detail. After all, if the modeller can observe such detail on the full-scale subject at the scale range then he, or she, must be able to simulate similar detail on the model. Thus a good model with a good paint finish can be a winner, and while a very good paint finish on a poor model will help it in some way, a bad finish on a good model will nevertheless put it at the bottom of the list.

INTRODUCTION TO THE AERO COLOUR TABLES (SEE APPENDIX 2)

The Colour Tables

This selection of some of the more generally used aero and AFV colours is in fact based upon close approximations of samples of *full-scale* colour found on original subjects, and are compared with those given in the *Methuen Handbook of Colour*. These measurements are then cross-referenced to the series of HUMBROL model paints.

However two important points must be appreciated by the reader. One, the Methuen book is one of the cheaper colour notation references on the market and, while being within the pocket of the average modeller, it does have certain limitations when trying to establish accurately very pale pastel blues and greys, and also when trying to establish very dark, fully saturated colours of deeper hues. Otherwise, the system when worked with a neutral coloured finder, can be extremely accurate and in any event, even when exact comparisons cannot be made, the hue graduations are such that the colour in question can be notated in a way that is considerably better than the well informed guess.

The second point is that paints are not necessarily always accurate in either title or in the colour that they are supposed to match, and variations in consistency fluctuate with shelf life and manufacturing batches in spite of rigid laboratory control at the factory. In this respect there is no substitute for a modeller collecting exact samples of

original colours and being able to mix his own model hues. This is particularly true where scale model paint values are being applied. Generally, such colour values should be reduced to the tint midway between the vertical colour columns in the Methuen book when the colour is being applied to 1/72nd scale models. For example, if the full-scale colour value is 4E8 then the scale colour should reduce halfway to D, giving 4(D−E)8 as the scale counterpart for the model.

In summing up the usefulness of the tables, readers are advised that the mixes given under the Humbrol Mix colours are offered only as a *guide* to achieving the full-scale colour and readers, in comparing the result with the Methuen value, may need to add small spots of other colours to reach the correct mix. Within the scope of these

tables it is not possible to give precise quantities because the quantities involved can be so small and as has already been stated, there can be differences in hue in the basic tinlets supplied. Few readers can perhaps buy a tin of *every* colour available, thus a mix may be achieved by using a different combination of colours which are the only ones the modeller has in stock. So the colours given are not necessarily the only method of arriving at the intended colour.

Therefore, when using the tables some discretion must be used as to how accurate a mix is required. One modeller may, for example, be happy to use Dark Green straight from the tin, whereas another, having compared that colour with the Methuen reference, may add a little black and yellow to get a more accurate mix.

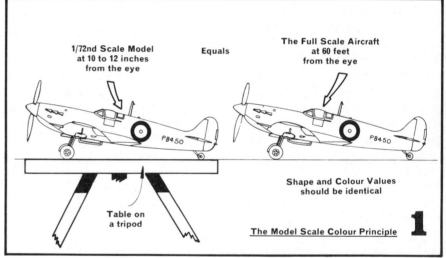

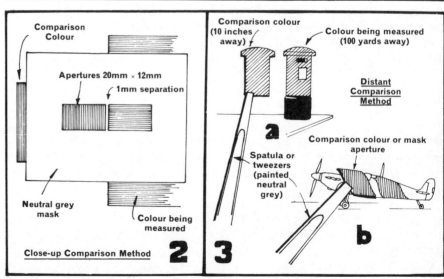

Mixing Hints & Tips

The mixing instructions given are those just sufficient to obtain a colour match, and are not necessarily sufficient to permit the painting of large areas of a model.

The 'parts' to e.g. '1 part No. 64 Light Grey' indicates one drop of paint from a standard eye-dropper, or one dip of a No. 2 size artist's sable brush, in a tinlet.

The 'dash' or 'spot' refers to roughly a quarter of a drop or just the tip of a No. 2 brush, dipped in the tinlet. It is usually easier to do the drops first using the eye-dropper and then add the dashes or spots with the paint brush after. However, if the modeller prefers, he can use the dropper in a 4:1 ratio, i.e. four drops for one part, and then add one drop for the dash or spot.

Once the colour value has been established, then larger quantities may then be mixed up according to the amount required on the model. Do keep notes and samples of all mixes, whether matched to tables, or to actual samples of fabric and metal. Filed in handy reference booklets, these colours become invaluable as time goes by, and so much time and effort is saved when it comes to the next model, when an exact mix can be quickly extracted from the reference.

Chapter 2

SCALE MODEL COLOUR AND METAL FINISH TECHNIQUES

The colour and appearance of a model can be either, or a mixture of, two things namely a natural or a synthetic finish, and it is necessary for the modeller to be able to simulate both with a fair amount of conviction. Whatever the finish or finishes may be, it is very important to be able to scale down both the *texture* and the *colour* of the full-scale subject.

Full-scale colour is quite correct for a full-scale replica but for smaller models the colour needs modification. The distance effect which causes this slight modification to the colours involved is due to the fact that in open space the colours slightly reflect both sky and surrounding terrain colouration, and also because the atmosphere is not wholly transparent. The same effect also causes what was a gloss surface in close-up to look only semi-gloss at range, so the general result is a paling and dulling of colours. Such model colour effects can be arrived at using a comparison method of matching similar sized samples, or by mixing and matching water colours much as the landscape artist would match his canvas to the distant scene. In other words, a small piece of colour at ten inches from the eye is matched against a similar sized area sixty feet from the eye and surprisingly the eye can soon adapt to focusing and refocusing a colour match

as soon as it has been reached.

Model scale colour should apply to *any* finish found on the full-scale subject whether it be a painted or a natural finished surface, and it is perhaps the latter finish, particularly when natural unpainted metals appear on aviation subjects, that in the past has not really been broken down into components that the modeller can fully appreciate. Thus the subject of silver airliners and military jet fighters are frequently given a wide berth, because the overall coat of silver paint definitely makes the model look wrong. Yet the metallic model finishes of today having been intermixed slightly are capable of producing a very effective finish which can be brushed on, as well as sprayed.

THE COLOUR OF METAL SKINNING

Generally aircraft are built from a mixture of aluminium, other light alloys, various steels and heat resisting alloys. The various metals themselves are produced to a variety of specifications and can be rolled sheet, cast or forged billets or machined from the slab components, each with a slightly differing surface finish and colouration. Sheet alloy appears in a variety of thicknesses, and usually the thinner the sheet the better the surface finish in order to resist corrosion. The commonest light alloy found is duralumin, which does not have good resistance to corrosion, so it is often coated with a thin layer of

Engine detail of author's Airfix B-29 Superfortress highlights differing tones of panels as described in the text. The picture also shows the thicker metal nose ring and cooling gills needing special treatment.

aluminium to improve both surface lustre and anti-corrosion properties.

The colours of these metals are basically silver-greys when new, dulling to slightly more greyish colours when worn. On a sunny airfield the surface lustre tends to reflect the sky and ground colouration making the metals adopt bluish-grey qualities.

The surfaces of airframe components are also broken up by panel and joint lines and a network of rivet lines and that, together with the differing hues of various metal, makes a patchwork quilt effect come to life. Add to this the dulled and blackened effects of jet pipes, and of oil and fuel stains particularly on the undersides of cowlings and fuselages, and it becomes obvious that a natural metal model cannot be represented by just giving it a coat of silver paint, or even by adding a few darker panels here and there!

Therefore three models facts appear:

Model Fact 1

Silver (aluminium) paint will only really represent a *painted aluminium* finish in full-scale (i.e. a wooden and fabric covered Mosquito, aluminium painted) and still needs the addition of a little light grey to represent the model colour.

Model Fact 2

Silver paint carefully mixed with other non-metallic paints can be made to be fairly representative of the multi-toned natural metal finish. The use of Brass and Gunmetal metallic paints in the same mixtures will together yield a series of five metal finishes which is about the minimum requirement for an effective metal finish.

Model Fact 3

Apply these five finishes to the model in an orderly sequence of some nine stages and the natural metal finish starts to become reality.

Suggested model metallic finishes

The basic ingredients upon which to draw for the mixes are taken from the Humbrol ranges of model paints and are as follows:

Table 1 Ingredients		
Article ref	Name	HUMBROL Reference
A	Airframe Silver	11
B	Silver Fox	11
C	Brass	54
D	Gunmetal	53
E	Hellblau 65	65
F	Leather	62
G	White	22 & 34
H	Black	21 & 33
I	Sea Grey Medium	64

Note: There is little to choose between the lustre of A or B. Gunmetal D, is rather dark and can be used neat for jet pipe areas.

COLOUR MIXES

The basic mixes should be arrived at by first putting a little well mixed Airframe Silver in a small palette and then adding the tinting colour in minute quantities at a time, thoroughly mixing the finish and testing the hue on a piece of scrap plastic each time.

Note: Having produced a set of the above hues as per table 2 which are only very slightly different in tone from one another, slightly darker or lighter mixes can be made to add to the range of metallic values. D + F + H will yield dark metallic finishes for the jet pipe in turbine interiors, and Gloss H will give a slightly oily look. By using separate matt white and gloss white in the light alloy mixes it will give additional tones for various panels and skin areas. A + G (matt) can be used for certain areas dulled by footsteps, on upper surfaces. (As experience is gained, so more metallic hues can be developed and used.)

METHOD OF APPLICATION

A much more satisfactory finish can result if all the components are painted *before* assembly. Dry fit all kit parts first so that only the minimum of fitting and filling is necessary during subsequent assembly.

If the kit parts are not moulded in grey plastic, or where extensive modifications have been effected, it is a good idea to give an overall undercoat of Sea Grey Medium 64 leaving it for at least twelve hours to harden before putting on another colour.

Carry out any extra surface detailing before commencing the painting of the

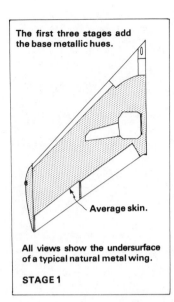

The first three stages add the base metallic hues.

Average skin.

All views show the undersurface of a typical natural metal wing.

STAGE 1

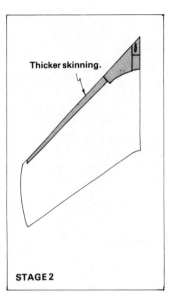

Thicker skinning.

STAGE 2

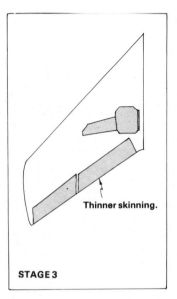

Thinner skinning.

STAGE 3

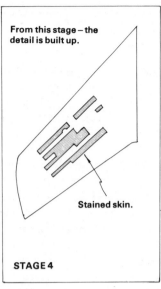

From this stage – the detail is built up.

Stained skin.

STAGE 4

top coats. Scribe additional skin joints and panel lines and if necessary chart up a skin drawing and roughly paint the areas as a guide to working on the actual model.

Before starting the metallic painting, ensure the kit parts are clean and dry (no dust or fingermarks) and aim to keep lightly loaded brush marks parallel to spars or the line of flight so that any imperfections would conform to full-scale blemishes. Lay on the metallic hue in the following order:

Stage 1 Brush in all the main areas in A + E for the average thickness skinning.

Stage 2 Add the darker areas in A + E + D for the thicker skinning.

Stage 3 Next add the lighter main areas in A + E + G. Generally flying control surfaces and flaps. (Stages 1 to 3 inclusive form the base colourings.)

Stage 4 This stage commences the surface detailing. Pick out certain underside panels in A + E + C where staining has taken place. Worn upper surface areas can be picked out with A + C.

Stage 5 Mark out all rivet lines in pure A using a ruling pen (or fine brush) in very fine lines over the whole of the airframe components.

Stage 6 Where necessary touch in contrasting rivet line colour where

Table 2 Metallic mixes

Metallic Mix	Proportions (approximate)	Description and use
A/B	Airframe Silver used neat	For certain small panels, but mainly to represent fine rivet lines.
A + E	3 of A to 1 of E	A silver grey with a faintly blue tinge, with less surface lustre than A. Used as a main base colour.
A + E + C	Add approx. 0.5 of C to A + E	As above but with a very slightly stained appearance. Used for certain undersurface areas.
A + E + D	Add approx. 0.5 of D to A + E	A darker alloy finish representing a heavier gauge metal. Darkened further represents steel jet pipe areas.
A + E + G	Add approx. 0.5 of G to A + E	A lighter alloy finish and for some rivet lines over stained skinning.

Note the way the different metal tones show up on the upper fuselage and wings. Reference to the table above indicates mixing of applicable shades.

lines have been lost to the base colour i.e. slightly darker over light and slightly lighter over dark.

Stage 7 Darker shadows can be applied to control surface hinge lines etc., panel edges and skin lines. Similar highlighting can follow that operation.

Stage 8 Add colour trim details, markings etc., and other final finishing details. Blend and weather all such detail and pick out screw heads in dark grey waterproof ink. Remember whites are usually too bright in national markings. Tone down with a duller colour.

Stage 9 Add oil stains and fresh dribbles running them over markings where appropriate. Add dark details to slots and vents in the airframe and add final weathering.

Observations

In the first instance all metallic hues should not be too strong or contrasting. Once the coatings have been applied check the visual appearance and add stronger or lighter tones if required. It is essential to keep the rivet lines as fine and accurate as possible.

Do work slowly and carefully on each panel as you come to them. They will reflect dim light very markedly and a panel with a wavy edge when it should be straight will look terrible. The patchwork quilt effect must look a precise pattern.

Remember oil residue is frequently wiped from airframes but it does leave a stain which blackens rivet heads and skin lines. These can be best marked in using a steel pen and waterproof brown or dark grey ink.

More engine nacelle detail seen above and below, careful brushwork is required to pick out the various panels helped immeasurably of course by moulded detail.

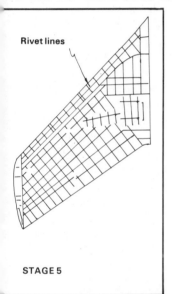

Rivet lines

STAGE 5

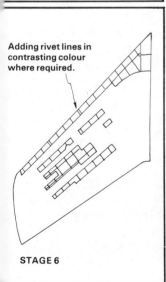

Adding rivet lines in contrasting colour where required.

STAGE 6

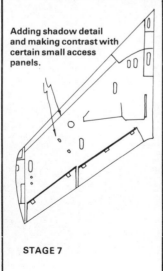

Adding shadow detail and making contrast with certain small access panels.

STAGE 7

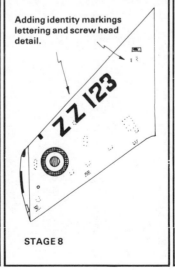

Adding identity markings lettering and screw head detail.

ZZ 123

STAGE 8

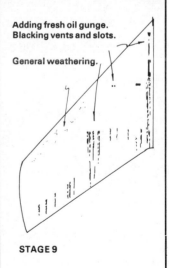

Adding fresh oil gunge. Blacking vents and slots.

General weathering.

STAGE 9

Chapter 3

METAL FINISHING THE SnJ WAY

The problem of how to obtain a natural metal finish on a plastic kit has long intrigued modellers. Over the years a variety of wondrous products has appeared that promised salvation. RUB 'n' BUFF paste was one of the earliest — anyone remember trying to use that? It was messy and tricky to handle but was an interesting alternative to old AIRFIX Silver paint which was about the only other option at the time. The HUMBROL metalcote paint is a much more recent product and in between we have had such innovations as chrome plating (see photo 1) and self-adhesive

foil (see photo 2). Some modellers have certainly achieved excellent results using one or other of the above items, but for many others including myself, the achievement of a really satisfactory metallic finish has proved elusive. Hence my interest in the SnJ *Spray Metal* system that has recently appeared from the USA.

In order to understand the value of this new product it is necessary to consider the problems encountered when using metallic paints of the orthodox type. One of these is that metallic paints tend to adhere to the model surface less

well than ordinary colours. Subsequently, if a metal finish is masked, the paint can often be lifted when the masking is removed. A further problem is that metallic paints form a poor base coat for successive colours, which can then be easily lifted themselves by masking materials. Also, many silver paints tend to have a rather 'grainy' finish when viewed close up, even if they have been applied by airbrush (see photo 3). A further problem is that metallic paints show up the slightest surface imperfections most ruthlessly, and consequently, a great deal of preparation

General view of the Otaki 1:48 scale P-47D Thunderbolt finished using the SnJ system.

work is required before the paint is applied.

The SnJ package is designed to overcome some of these problems. A good place to start, not surprisingly is the *Starter Kit*, which consists of two 1oz bottles of paint, a 5/8oz jar of polishing powder and a 5/8oz mixing bottle. Also provided is a polishing cloth and a comprehensive set of instructions. This route is more costly, and it is possible to buy a single bottle of paint and the polishing powder separately if you want to keep the cost down (see photo 4). Even so, this paint certainly isn't cheap and after paying this sort of price expectations would be high.

THE MODEL

There were several kits to hand that were suitable for a natural metal finish. In the end the 1:48 scale Thunderbolt, produced by OTAKI and now available under the ARII label was selected. This is a well moulded and well fitting kit which goes together with little trouble, allowing the final painting stage to be arrived at quickly. The kit goes together well, with only small amounts of filling and sanding required around the major

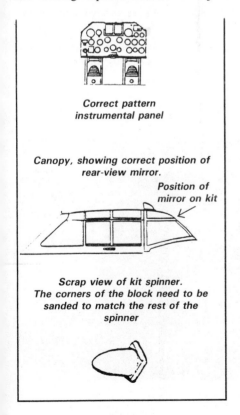

Correct pattern instrumental panel

Canopy, showing correct position of rear-view mirror.

Position of mirror on kit

Scrap view of kit spinner. The corners of the block need to be sanded to match the rest of the spinner

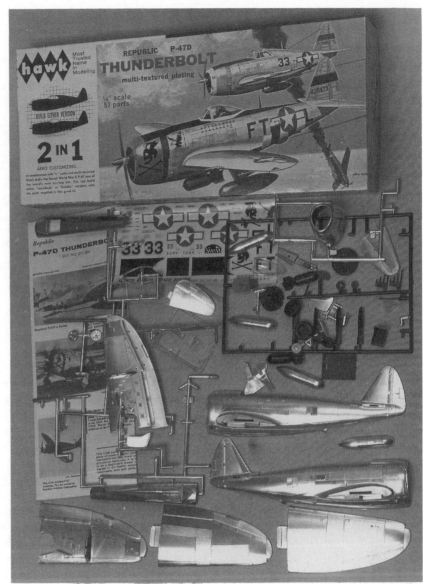

Photo 1: The Hawk P-47D kit of 1964 featured plated parts and a variety of surface texture. An interesting idea, but much of the plating would be lost in the building process.

joints, although there was a surprising number of 'sink' marks that needed attention on both wings and fuselage.

The Finish

One of the problems with a metal finish that SnJ won't solve is the need for the surface to be completely free of blemishes and imperfections. A long time was spent working with wet and dry paper of the finest grade and finishing off with metal polish. Even then, some faults were shown up by the first coat of paint, and more work was necessary. The SnJ instructions are clear and comprehensive. No priming is required,

so painting can begin as soon as the surfaces have been sufficiently cleaned up. The paint can only be applied by airbrush but those with top-mounted colour cups rather than bottom-mounted jars are not recommended in the instructions as the metal pigment tends to settle too quickly to the bottom of the cup, causing clogging. Despite this a Badger 150 with side cup was used and no particular problems were encountered, although I must be the first to admit that it was only used for a short space of time. The rest of the work was carried out using a DE VILBISS Super 63. Obviously bottom cup/bottle airbrushes such as the BADGER 200 and 350 or

15

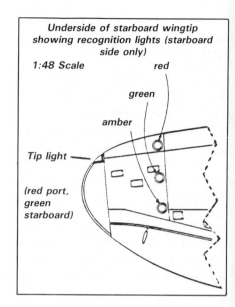

Photo 2: A Thunderjet finished in silver enamel and thin aluminium foil. This is one method of achieving
a variety of shine and texture.

the DE VILBISS Sprite Major are best suited to this product.

The paint does not have to be thinned. It has to be 'misted' on in three or four coats, with a ten to fifteen minute delay between each one. If you apply too much at once it results in a rather strange glazed appearance that is not at all desirable. If the model is a large one, the instructions recommend that painting is carried out one section at a time. Once the coats have been applied, they take about an hour to dry giving a semi-gloss aluminium finish. This looks good, but it can be improved further.

To get the extra shine, the instructions tell you to buff the model with a soft cloth. This was tried, and although it resulted in some extra shine, it was much easier to use the polishing powder. A small amount of powder was applied to the section of the model with a spatula. This was then polished with the cloth and a very effective burnished finish resulted. By using varying amounts of powder and polishing, it is easy to obtain a wide range of different tones on the various panels of the model. Further changes can be rung by adding touches of gloss enamel to the basic silver paint, but this technique wasn't actually tried on this model.

At this stage, it begins to become apparent that this SnJ product is very good. The paint covers well and is remarkably smooth — no 'grain' effect

is visible at all. With a bit of polishing, an excellent metallic lustre is obtained that looks most effective. A real wonder of the stuff is that unlike any other silver finish previously used, it can be easily masked. This is a great help when working on different adjacent panels, and when additional colours are added on top of the SnJ, it takes them very well. The red cowling band and yellow rudder were put on over the metal finish with no problems at all. Decals proved to be no trouble either. Using a combination of SUPERSCALE and the thicker kit items, both adhered well. The setting solutions (the old Microsol,

Microset and their current equivalents, and Decalfix) had no detrimental effect on the finish.

Some words of caution may be in order at this stage. Firstly, while the paint is largely immune to damage by masking, it was found that areas polished to a very high shine did have some of the brilliance dulled by masking tape used roughly. Secondly, after an area has been polished using the powder, make sure sufficient time is allowed for it to cure (the instructions recommend at least 12 hours) otherwise it can be marked by fingerprints that cannot easily be polished away.

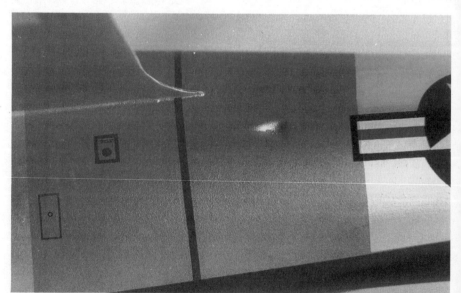

Photo 3: A close inspection of the Thunderjet shows the rather 'grainy' finish of the paint compared to
the smooth foil.

Thirdly, when using the powder, avoid spilling it on transparencies or areas of non metallic colour. It will mark if not removed very carefully. Finally, attention must be drawn to the important note in the instructions that a protective mask must be worn while using the polishing powder to avoid inhaling the dust.

Conclusion

The results obtained with this product were most impressive and our high expectations of it were largely fulfilled. It is the best metallic paint I have used and even my first attempt with it yielded encouraging results. With practice, I think even better things could be achieved, and I have already seen some excellent models finished using this system. Although the starter pack is expensive there is a lot of paint and powder provided — I used only about a tenth of the total on the Thunderbolt model shown on the previous page. If, like me, you have had difficulties with metal finishes in the past, the SnJ paint system is certainly worth a try.

Sources

The SnJ Starter Pack was bought from E.D. Models of 64, Stratford Road, Shirley, Solihull, West Midlands. SnJ products can also be obtained from Hannants, 29—31 Trafalgar Street, Lowestoft, Suffolk.

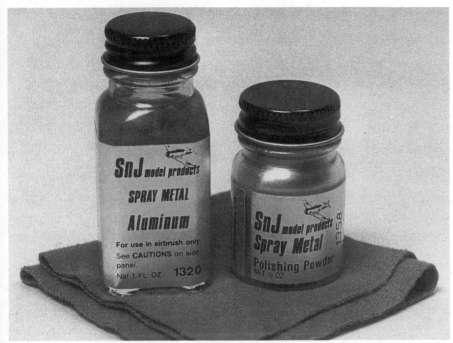
Photo 4: The SnJ System — spray paint, polishing powder and polishing cloth.

Chapter 4

PAINTING: HINTS AND TIPS

THE TOOLS

Brushes

When you stop to consider that the painting of any scale model is quite often the most demanding and time-consuming aspect of modelling, it is surprising that relatively few tools are required. One thing that must be stressed is that it is false economy to buy cheap tools whether brushes, spray guns or other types of accessory. The first move should be to purchase a varied selection of good quality sable brushes from an artists' supplier who could be expected to stock only the very best.

Although the sable brush is quite expensive, if properly looked after it will outlive most other types as the bristles are somewhat more resilient.

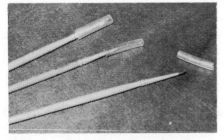

The size of brush is also an important factor and surprisingly it is not always the case that the '0' or '00' size are the best choice for very small details. A good No. 2 sable with the tip slightly dampened before painting often gives superior results as the larger bristle is easier to handle.

Sizes ranging from '00' to No. 10 would cover most plastic modellers' needs with perhaps one or two fine lining, chisel or stencil brushes to complete the selection. However many brushes you have, it is essential to look after them properly both during and after use.

No brush should *ever* be used to stir paint as nothing will remove the hairs quicker, neither should any one brush be used for all jobs. Each ought to be reserved for particular applications and marked clearly as such. Never leave the brushes to soak in thinners either, but clean them thoroughly in white spirit, then wipe the brush on a clean soft, lint-free cloth, or good quality soft tissue, (kitchen or toilet!). If you use the same brush for different colours, you should have three small bottles (old mustard jars are ideal) filled with thinners, or suitable solvents to hand. Use the first to get most of the paint from the brush, the second to rinse out and the third as a final dip before carefully wiping off. To protect the hairs afterwards, use a short length of plastic tubing slipped over the metal shank. Many artists' brushes are available with these ready fitted, but alternatives are easily found in the form of model aircraft neoprene fuel tubing. This can be bought in various diameters and chopped up to provide durable sheaths.

Finally, the brushes should be stored in an airtight container such as an old pencil box — never store them upright or leave them standing in a jar of thinners.

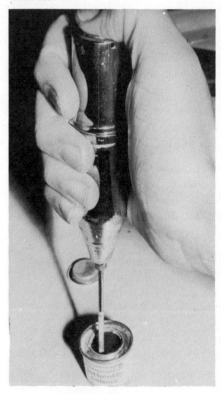

Paint Stirrers

The thorough mixing of proprietary model paints is very important and small lengths of metal rod or scrap sprue can be used to break up any lumps and for general stirring. Do *not* use wooden cocktail sticks or similar as these can splinter and the fragments will enter the paint. A speedier method is to use a battery-powered cocktail stirrer with the 'blade' suitably cut down to act as a small 'propeller'. This should not be switched on until the shank is well into the paint, otherwise you could well get smothered!

Thinners

All paint ranges, whether cellulose or enamel, provide recommended thinners and for the latter ordinary white spirit is sufficient. Old discarded washing-up liquid plastic bottles are ideal for storing thinners (enamel only) as they can hold a considerable amount and the flip-up top controls the liquid. If fitted with a length of neoprene tubing, a good measure of directional control is also obtained. More potent solvents can often be used to distinct advantage, and chemicals such as M.E.K. benzine, cellulose thinner and the like, should only be stored in glass bottles or metal cans. Many modern acrylics have their own specialist thinners and some newer paints are water-based. It pays, therefore, to keep all thinner and solvent containers clearly labelled to avoid the disaster of incorrect use.

Palettes

The mixing of colours should be done in small containers, such as old eggcups, or shallow food container lids, but choose materials made from metal or china so that there is no chance of them being affected by any paint or dope. These palettes can also be used to hold standard paints poured from a tin; an opened tinlet should not be exposed to the air for long as this will have adverse effects upon the contents. This is especially so with matt paints which dry out fairly rapidly and the use of the palette means the tinlets can be resealed almost immediately. Make sure the paint tin is firmly shut, and do not allow paint to build up around the edges of the rim otherwise an airtight seal cannot be made. The transfer of paint from tin to palette or airbrush is sometimes difficult due to tin design, for the paint tends to collect in the rim around the lid and is difficult to remove. Old medical syringes, with the needle removed, could be used to transfer enamel and are easily cleaned with spirit afterwards. Proops Bros are a source of small nylon syringes ideal for this use.

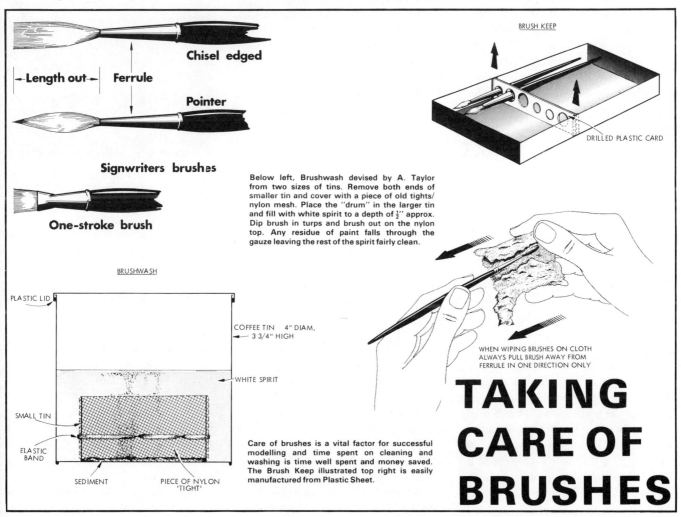

Chisel edged

Pointer

— Length out — Ferrule

Signwriters brushes

One-stroke brush

BRUSH KEEP

DRILLED PLASTIC CARD

Below left, Brushwash devised by A. Taylor from two sizes of tins. Remove both ends of smaller tin and cover with a piece of old tights/nylon mesh. Place the "drum" in the larger tin and fill with white spirit to a depth of ½" approx. Dip brush in turps and brush out on the nylon top. Any residue of paint falls through the gauze leaving the rest of the spirit fairly clean.

BRUSHWASH

PLASTIC LID

COFFEE TIN 4" DIAM.
— 3 3/4" HIGH

WHITE SPIRIT

SMALL TIN

ELASTIC BAND

SEDIMENT

PIECE OF NYLON 'TIGHT'

WHEN WIPING BRUSHES ON CLOTH ALWAYS PULL BRUSH AWAY FROM FERRULE IN ONE DIRECTION ONLY

Care of brushes is a vital factor for successful modelling and time spent on cleaning and washing is time well spent and money saved. The Brush Keep illustrated top right is easily manufactured from Plastic Sheet.

TAKING CARE OF BRUSHES

Masking Materials

We will be dealing with masking in depth later on, but for standard brushing, masking material, though important, is not used quite as often.

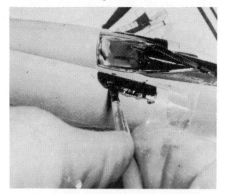

SCOTCH TAPE or even SELLO-TAPE is often used by many modellers to obtain sharp delineation between two colours such as upper and lower surfaces of a warplane. One way to guarantee a really sharp line is to press the tape *firmly* onto the required area having first run the fingers over the sticky side to remove most of the tackiness, otherwise when removed this could remove the base coat. Before applying the paint, dip a clean cloth in white spirit and rub *gently* along the edge in a single swipe. This serves to clean out any minute portions of the tape adhesive and prevents any gaps in between masking tape and painting area. You must ensure that the tape is quite secure before applying paint and that the thinners have had sufficient time to dry off before painting.

Perhaps having greater advantage is proper masking tape, a buff-coloured opaque variety with a not too vicious backing adhesive. The advantage of this material is that it can be used for compound curves without kinking — something that on occasions Sellotape is unable to do. If placed on a sheet of glass, thin strips can be cut using a sharp knife guided by a metal straight-edge and the strips used to obtain lines or even large numerals. Quite complex curves can be made using this sort of tape and it is also to be recommended for masking areas prior to using the airbrush. Specialist tapes — such as those produced for designers of printed

circuit boards — available from the better stocked graphics dealers, offer a similar route. Usually black in colour, they are made from the same crêpe paper and are available from as thin as 10 thou (0.01″) up to 2″ in both imperial and metric sizes. Precise cut tapes like this enable specific width lines to be painted.

Liquid masking material is available commercially in several forms, but PVA Adhesive such as that manufactured by Deluxe Materials, Evo Stick, D B Models and Humbrol is just as good. Similarly, thinned down Copydex works well. The use of such liquids is

somewhat limited for normal brushing techniques, for masking off camouflage areas by hand with masking material is no different from applying the colour direct to the model; where it scores is in masking canopies and general duties when using spray equipment. Canopies can be liberally covered in the glue and left to harden before painting. It is easily removed later by lifting a corner and ripping off, but more of that later...

Ruling Pens

For the real enthusiast, ruling pens can find many uses, especially if one has separate ink bows attachments for a pair of compasses, and the pens can take nearly all types of paint provided it is thinned sufficiently and applied carefully. Used with a straight-edge tilted 45 degrees to the model straight sharp cheat lines can be applied and with a pair of compasses the handpainting of aircraft roundels becomes extremely simple. After painting thin concentric rings with the inkbow, the 'middles' can be filled in with a fine brush, the centres being done last. Skilled modellers can even use these tools to create numerals

and letters, but considerable practice is required before moving on to such niceties.

Rags

A selection of lint-free cloths or tissues are useful to have handy for wiping brushes and keeping the hands clean. Any spillage too can be quickly mopped up without the risk of this getting on clothing or parts of the model. This completes the list of basic tools and we can now consider other matters.

Paints

There are many ranges of model enamels readily available and most are of high quality. Ranges such as those of Humbrol, Pactra, Revell, Hannants, Tamiya and Testors all provide a large number of standard colours as well as authentic military colours.

Epoxy paints such as those shown—are usually considered totally fuel proof.

PREPARATION

These enamels can be applied to almost any kind of scale model whether wood, metal or plastic, once the particular surface has been initially prepared. On models that require powering by diesel or glow plug engines such as flying model aircraft or speed boats, the enamels need fuel proofing either by commercially marketed fuel proofer or polyurethanes.

After compiling the necessary amount of reference material and before you

A selection of the major ranges of model enamel available on the market today. Revell, Pactra, Testors, Humbrol and Airfix each produce an extensive range of matt and gloss colours.

even think of applying the main colour to a plastic model, you must first check to see whether the surface is clean. We make no excuses for stressing the absolute necessity for a clean painting surface. It may seem obvious to remind you to remove joint lines, excess cement and prime filler material, but it is surprising to see models completely painted without any attempt to smooth these areas over.

Glue should always be left to dry *before* attempting to remove it, preferably with a craft knife, and never moved while setting. Coarse sandpaper as such should be deemed unnecessary on plastic models, as wet and dry paper is to be preferred. This should be kept quite well soaked and soap can also be used with the water to get a finer finish. All joint lines gaps etc. should be filled prior to painting and although many brands of proprietary model fillers are available, choose with care. INTERNAL POLYFILLA is perhaps one of the best materials to use on plastic models. It is water soluble, does not affect the surrounding plastic and is easily sanded. SQUADRON GREEN STUFF is perhaps one of the better commercial products. Prior to painting the model, the filler, having been smoothed, is coated with two coats of enamel of a neutral colour to seal the filler and present a smooth finish for final painting.

In general most plastic kits do not require a coat of primer prior to painting unless you are spraying a cellulose finish in which case the plastic needs a protective coat of lacquer such as FRISK LAC GLOSS. Failure to do this will have the result of the cellulose crazing and wrinkling the plastic surface. (Not so with airbrushing — see later.)

On flying model aircraft, or other forms of model utilising balsa wood in its construction, then this must first be finished with sanding sealer. Usually two or three coats are needed, sanding with fine flour paper between coats and a really smooth finish needs to be obtained before you can even think of painting the model. Alternatively, modern polyester or epoxy finishing resins offer a good, quick route.

Having filled, sanded and smoothed your model it should be cleaned of all greases and sanding dust by first flicking off with a brush and then washing with warm water to which mild detergent is added. Then final dust, specks etc. can be finally removed by using an anti-static cloth, such as that used for cleaning LP records. After this the model must be handled carefully while painting takes place.

THE TECHNIQUES

We are going to assume that you have already read Chapter 1 Introduction and that you have all the materials and the model to hand right now. We are also going to assume that any joint lines have been filled and smoothed down with wet and dry fine grade paper. Dust and grease should have been removed by gently washing the model in lukewarm water to which a little mild detergent has been added. Thereafter handle the model with care, gripping it only with a scrap of paper between

fingers otherwise grease will take a hold. A pair of light cotton gloves could also be used.

General Application

What size or shape of brush you elect to use is, of course, dependent on the model subject. Enamels are easy to apply using one of the medium sables, and should present few problems if care is taken. Only small quantities should be brushed on at a time, keeping the brush moving in one direction only. If the paint does not cover well after the first coat, resist the temptation to go back over it and remember the old maxim — *two thin coats are better than one thick one*. Sharp defined edges such as a leading edge colour demarcation should be lightly brushed along their length using the edge of the brush in some areas. Remember to keep all brush strokes in one direction. At least *six hours* should elapse before a second coat is applied and even longer if a third is needed.

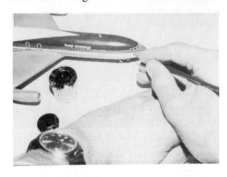

While painting it is useful to support your hand, especially if there is a tricky shape to negotiate. Small blocks of wood or a stout box lid can hold the model while the painting hand is rested on the other to steady the brush. Finally, leave the model to dry in a dust-free atmosphere wherever this is possible.

Having dispensed with broad generalities it may be helpful if certain difficult areas that often prove troublesome to beginners are individually discussed along with the techniques to overcome them.

Pre-painting

In many of today's more sophisticated

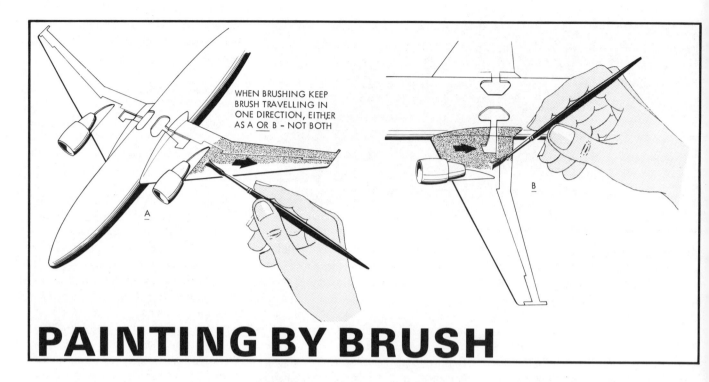

WHEN BRUSHING KEEP BRUSH TRAVELLING IN ONE DIRECTION, EITHER AS A OR B - NOT BOTH

A

B

PAINTING BY BRUSH

plastic kits you will find a multitude of small and delicate pieces which will be tricky to paint. Therefore you have to decide the best way to tackle these and there is a lot to be said for painting the parts while still attached to the sprues. Naturally the whole frame must be washed first, but having done that you will find painting these smaller parts immeasurably easier by having a convenient handhold. When dry the items can be carefully removed with a craft knife and the small area of unpainted plastic revealed can be simply touched in, remembering of course to avoid painting any areas that will require cement.

Wheels

On larger scale cars and certain prestigious aircraft kits, tyres are moulded in rubber but painting small plastic wheels is never very easy, unless tackled in the correct manner. A cocktail stick is pushed through the centre and the tyre carefully painted by rotating the stick between forefinger and thumb, holding the brush with the other hand. The technique can be used for painting both hub and tyre and while drying the other end of the cocktail stick can be inserted into a block of

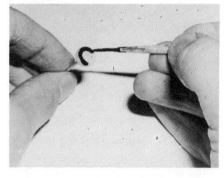

Plasticine. As certain kit wheels do not have their centres pierced right through, the cocktail stick must be trimmed until it is a tight fit.

Another obvious, but often over-looked, factor governing realism in painting tyres is the actual colour of them. Look carefully at any wheeled

vehicle using inflatable rubber tyres and they will look more grey than black. Thus for rubber tyres do not accept the kit instructions — if they state black, instead use dark grey which looks more authentic. After the paint has dried, you can gently rub the tread area with a soft cloth to represent wear.

Transparencies

Perhaps one of the trickiest operations is painting the framelines to aircraft cockpit canopies and glazed gun turrets. Whichever one of several methods you adopt it becomes immeasurably easier if the transparency is painted *before* attaching to the model.

Handpainting. If the canopy has raised

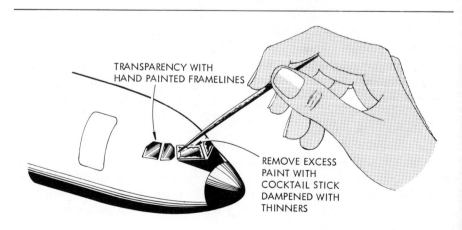

TRANSPARENCY WITH HAND PAINTED FRAMELINES

REMOVE EXCESS PAINT WITH COCKTAIL STICK DAMPENED WITH THINNERS

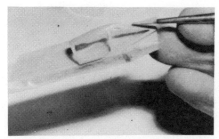

Handholds and/or support of the brush are vital for tricky operations such as colouring wheels and canopy frames.

or sunken lines these can be painted on by hand using one of the finer sizes of brush such as 0 or No. 1. For ease the part can be mounted on a piece of double-sided Sellotape which in turn is placed on a piece of scrap wood thus serving as a useful handhold. This serves a dual purpose as besides being easier to handle, it also prevents any paint encroaching onto the main gluing area. At least two coats is usually needed and even the most skilled modeller will find the paint has overlapped the framework. If not left to harden, the unwanted excess can be removed with a sharpened cocktail stick dipped in thinners.

Masking. A time-consuming method is to mask off the full-scale clear area with liquid masking to leave the framelines untouched. When satisfied every corner is filled and the glue dried, the whole canopy can be sprayed or brushed, and on removing the masking, the framelines should stand in relief. Any touching up can be done later by fine brush.

A useful tip here is to cover the entire canopy with masking fluid, (you can colour PVA or Copydex with cochineal, pinched from the cooking cupboard so that you can see where you are going). When dry, use a sharp scalpel to cut the edges of the fluid mask using the raised/indented frame edges as a guide. Pull off the area to be painted. This method produces sharper edges than can be painted by hand.

Painted strips. Thin adhesive tape can be painted in the desired colour, cut into strips and applied by tweezers. A really flexible tape is needed to follow any awkward contour, and the only drawback is that the self-adhesive backing may become weak in time. To be truly accurate the insides of canopies should have the frames painted in the cockpit interior colour, but this is very difficult and one must decide how important this is, before trying it.

Natural Metal Finishes

Painting. It was disappointing, having beaten the problem of applying an overall coat of silver, to complete a model and then realise that something vital was still lacking. The trouble was that full-size aircraft are made up from separate panels and all the pieces vary to a greater or lesser extent in appearance. Sometimes it is because the stock material has come from different sup-

pliers, or has slight surface texture differences, or where distinct colours show up it may be that special alloys are used for strength at highly stressed points, or to resist heat, as in the case of the titanium to be seen at the tail of a Phantom.

Within limits it is easy to alter the look of silver paints by mixing in small amounts of black or white and experiments with plastic models have shown if four shades of silver are used after careful reference to photographs, there is a definite improvement.

The drawing of an F-100D was made up from several pictures and it was obvious while doing it that panels might look relatively pale on one aircraft while on another example the same ones could be dark. Nevertheless, the drawing was a compromise to produce the general effect on a model, accepting the fact that probably no two machines are the same.

Of the four silvers one is straight from the tin, one has a little white in it, the other two have black to modify them, and a special very dark mix is brewed for the tail pipe.

The mix. Find a piece of scrap metal or plastic sheet and divide it into four patches, and paint the second patch with silver as it comes from the tin. At the same time paint all the parts of model shown as *Silver-2*. Now put about eight

NATURAL METAL FINISH TONES

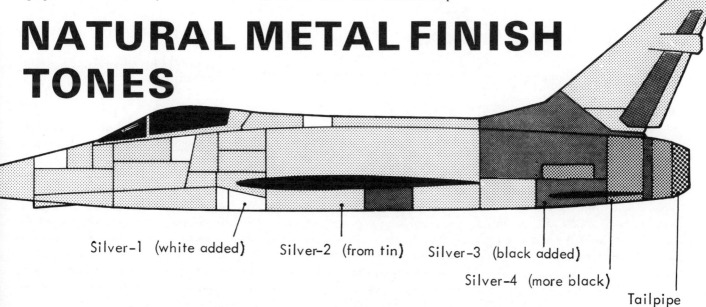

Silver-1 (white added) Silver-2 (from tin) Silver-3 (black added)
Silver-4 (more black)
Tailpipe

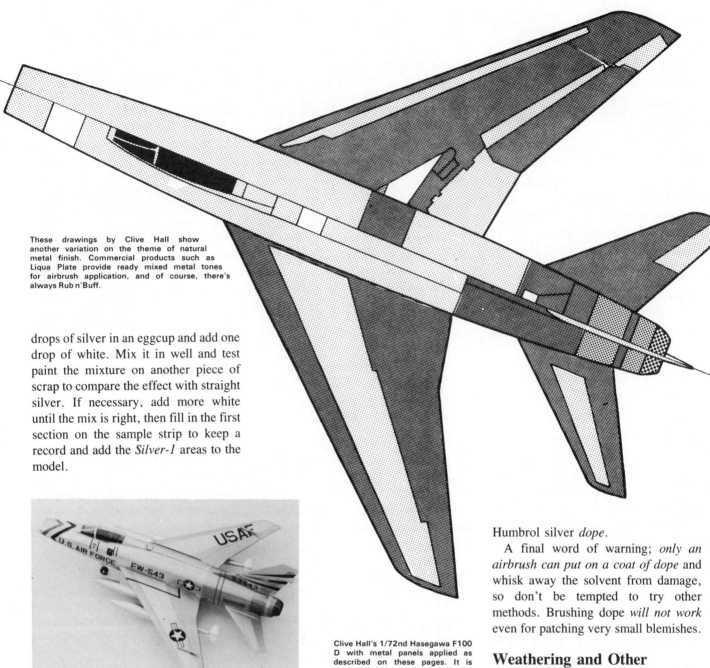

These drawings by Clive Hall show another variation on the theme of natural metal finish. Commercial products such as Liqua Plate provide ready mixed metal tones for airbrush application, and of course, there's always Rub n'Buff.

drops of silver in an eggcup and add one drop of white. Mix it in well and test paint the mixture on another piece of scrap to compare the effect with straight silver. If necessary, add more white until the mix is right, then fill in the first section on the sample strip to keep a record and add the *Silver-1* areas to the model.

Clive Hall's 1/72nd Hasegawa F100 D with metal panels applied as described on these pages. It is obvious just how effective the differing tones appear.

The remaining two silvers, modified with black, can be treated in the same way in turn, *Silver-4*, in fact, can be made by putting more black with *Silver-3*, keeping a continual check on the effect produced by the additions. The tailplane colour is made from silver and black with some yellow and red. Only a little is wanted so start with one drop of each and adjust to the correct burnt-metal tone.

If an airbrush finish is contemplated the quality of the surface should be first-class, but there is a masking problem which can be formidable and it will make life easier to prepare all the shades first and to work in the order 4-3-1-2 after first finishing the tailplane. For the best results it is possible to use cellulose although it can be most difficult to mask, sticking as it does to the tape and not to the model. It can, however, be made to work if Humbrol gloss enamel is first sprayed overall as a primer. The model illustrated is from the kit by HASEGAWA and is finished in Humbrol silver *dope*.

A final word of warning; *only an airbrush can put on a coat of dope* and whisk away the solvent from damage, so don't be tempted to try other methods. Brushing dope *will not work* even for patching very small blemishes.

Weathering and Other Techniques

Drybrushing. Just painting the model in its correct scale colours is usually still not enough to give an overall authentic finish and you must seek to bring out the moulded detail prevalent on today's bigger kits, such as exposed engines on aircraft and tank models. Drybrushing is one way to achieve weathering effects on models and is described below as an operation for a wartime vehicle although different colours and materials can be used for other models as further paragraphs reveal.

EASY PAINT TRANSFERENCE TO PALETTE OR AIRBRUSH

TRANSFERRING PAINT
TO PALETTE BY USE OF SYRINGE

PALETTE

Having already painted the vehicle in the correct colours the model should be left to dry before spraying or brushing on a matt varnish such as DULLCOTE EXTRA FLAT or any other of the proprietary matt finish products. Their purpose is to prevent removal of the base colour while drybrushing the weathering colour, and like most finishes these should be left to harden for at least 24 hours.

For vehicles the model then has a very thinned down wash applied of dark grey water colour, or even watered-down drawing ink, to deaden the base colour and fill in the moulded panel lines thus serving to further accentuate them. When this has dried, actual drybrushing can commence and a stiff, nylon brush is used. The paint used for weathering is best applied by mixing a little light grey or even white with the base colour and this should be fairly thick. The brush is dipped into it and run over scrap paper until only the tip holds any colour and very little of it at that. The brush is then gently flicked over the whole model several times so that all moulded detail is caught by the colour, while the remainder retains its base coat. One could use another darker shade to go over other areas but a word of caution — do not overload the brush and do not overdo the drybrushing technique either. Dark Earth or Sand can also be drybrushed to types of vehicles or aircraft to give a weathered effect and perhaps water-based paints offer a greater advantage here.

Aircraft represent a challenge to the modeller, especially where weathering is concerned, and various techniques are described throughout this book, although here we are only concerned with drybrushing. The method adopted above by using a lighter colour drybrushed over the base colour is used to good effect in fuselage interiors where there is added detail to these areas. Stringer and panel lines can be accentuated in this manner and if the colour is gradually darkened towards the floor of the fuselage, a feeling of depth is also achieved.

Engines and wheel hubs look effective if drybrushed with a Dark Grey/Silver mix, but please do not use straight silver as it is far too bright. Engines can be further improved by an additional wash of Dark Grey colour leaving a glossy effect — never paint such components Matt Black as is so often (and incorrectly) recommended. Drybrushing techniques can be applied (but, very faintly) to highlight surface panel detail on aircraft by again using the lighter colour, but to look effective should *only* be applied in one specific direction — *chordwise* on wings and tailplanes, *vertically* on fuselages.

How to apply highlights. Above left, the basic model component in its base colour in this instance, a 1/28th scale rotary engine. Above right, aluminium paint is "brushed out" onto paper so only a minimum is retained on the brush. Far left, this is flicked over the model part, and the small amounts of paint just catching the detail bring it out into relief as in the final picture.

Thinned-down ink can further be used to accentuate control surfaces by running paint into the moulded joint lines, thus serving to emphasise these areas on separate components but, the tones should always be carefully mixed — again avoiding pure black or pure white. Which type of paint you use for these effects is purely a matter of choice, acrylics or water-based colours can be applied over dry medium without fear of damage, but if using enamel don't forget the matt varnish coat finish

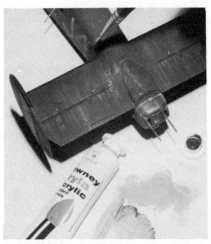

Applying highlights to moulded surface detail of a Liberator. Water based paints are used so as not to affect the basic enamel finish.

to protect the base colour.

Finally, do not try and simulate chips and scratches by drybrushing over panels and leading edges — this does not look right at all and such weathering is only convincing if the 'silver' chips are individually handpainted. Remember again that the drybrushing technique should be applied with restraint, something that is quite difficult for some people to realise, for once they see how effective the process looks, they are tempted to go over it again with greater emphasis — *don't*.

Highlighting. The drybrushing technique as previously described is not the only way to add a realistic impression to a model. With this in mind, however, many models are spoilt by lack of thought to the result aimed for, as highlighting such as outlines of under-carriage doors or inspection panels is not quite the same as drybrushing to get a weathered effect. Firstly, the basic

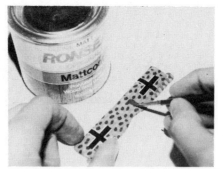

Polyurethane varnish gives a durable and lasting protective (and fuel proof) finish to all types of model. Airbrushing however, is to be recommended.

rules are literally to get the brush almost dry and not to overload this, as it is better to have too little a result after application than too much. Finally *never* use white or black as a means of highlighting for these are too harsh a contrast. Instead use various tones of grey or, if working on a tank model in desert finish, use a slightly darker tone than the base colour. For example, if the model was a Matilda Tank in overall Humbrol 8th Army Desert Yellow, use Mid Stone, and/or Dark Earth. For a weathered appearance use a tone also darker than the base colour(s), except where dust or desired mud effects are sought, in which case use a lighter tone, such as Humbrol Khaki Drill or Humbrol Concrete — drybrushed of course. If you choose to use an airbrush, hold a piece of thin card about two inches from the model area to be 'dusted' (i.e. tank track, running gear)

etc. to avoid any hard demarcation lines. The golden rule for these types of effects is too little can be rectified, too much cannot.

VARNISHING

Having painted the model to your satisfaction and added decals, you may find that either due to poor mixing or room temperature or whatever, some of the painted areas have an uneven sheen i.e. Dark Earth colour on an aircraft might not be quite as matt as its Dark

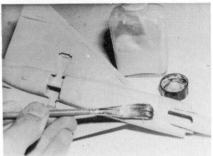

A coat of liquid polystyrene cement helps to seal plastic and filler prior to painting.

Green neighbour. Similarly decals might also present a different appearance. Therefore you have to try to obtain an overall smooth finish dependant of course on the model subject, and this takes the form of matt and gloss clear varnishes and any of the satins, semi-matts etc. in between. These are usually best sprayed on, but, with one

---

VARNISH COMPATIBILITY
TABLE OF BASIC TYPES OF MODEL FINISH

TYPES	MANUFACTURER	REMARKS
Polyurethanes: Matt Gloss Satin	Ronseal,* Kingston Diamond,* Translac,* Humbrol,* Coverite,* Crown,* etc	Gives superb overall finish over enamels, dopes, decals etc. Does not need to be sprayed due to excellent covering characteristics. Also used as fuel proofer for flying model aircraft.
Varnishes: Matt Gloss	Humbrol, Joy, also Fuel Proofers etc.	Not quite as good a finish as one might quite expect, useful though for attaching fine parts or filling fine joints. Also used as fuel proofer for flying model aircraft.
Lacquer: Matt Gloss	Frisk Lac*	Mostly Aerosol. Gives excellent flat finish on plastic aircraft and tanks and gloss on large-scale cars (and can also be used over enamels and decals).
Spray Varnishes:	Micro scale: (USA)* (A) Dullcote/glosscote*	Only to be applied by airbrush, assists decal finishing. Can be used over enamels and decals or plastic models.

*Use mark when applying by spray.

or two exceptions, can safely only be used with a standard brush. The Varnish Compatibility table lists most of the major types of clear finish and which are compatible with each other.

The application of any clear finishing coats demands just as much care and attention as any other operation and should not be rushed in any instance. What type of finish you apply depends really on the availability of the particular finish chosen and if you have an airbrush, which is used for some types. Polyurethanes should be *brushed on* and only sprayed when there is adequate ventilation and most important of all, when *you use a face mask*.

If spraying a clear coat, all transparent areas should first be masked off and it is most important that before applying any clear varnish, the paint and decals have been left to dry for at least twenty-four hours. On most WW2 aircraft, a flat finish was seen, although some aircraft had special 'waxed' finishes for extra speed. Glossy colours are common on many modern aircraft but on the model an eggshell finish usually looks better.

Chapter 5

EARLY AIRCRAFT –
SOME GUIDANCE

Veteran and vintage aircraft subjects (for me this covers anything from 1939 backwards) present interesting challenges to the modelling enthusiast, not the least of which is the hoary old controversial topic of World War One colours and markings. This is a vast complex subject, that confuses many people and probably is a reason why WW1 aircraft kits are not too popular with the majority of modellers. This is especially relevant when you consider that few really accurate and comprehensive references on the subject are available.

The purpose here is to provide just a basic guide to painting models of early aircraft and can in no way be

claimed as the 'last word'. WW1 shades in the colour table have been based on surviving fabric samples cross referenced with the Methuen *Book of Colour*.

Actual markings and insignia are

really beyond the scope of this short chapter. Instead what follows are a few guides to painting and weathering applicable to early aircraft, whether plastic non-flying or large flying wood models.

Above: author's 1/72nd scale BE2c painted in 'clear' finish and PC10 Brown mixed to specifications in the Aero Colour Table. Right: this Nieuport 16 features the early two colour camouflage for French WW1 aircraft and carries wraparound upper colour borders on the undersurfaces.

GENERALITIES

'Fabric Weave' Finish

On a great many early aircraft kits where fabric-covered areas are represented, manufacturers have applied a coarse fabric weave finish which is of course pure nonsense in my view. The weave is not readily visible, even on the full-size aircraft, having been filled by dope and so there is no excuse for representing it on any small scale model. Where this is found it should be removed by gentle sanding using wet and dry paper.

Tyres

In general most aircraft tyres from 1907 onwards were grey and in some cases a very light shade, and in others even white! So *never* paint the tyres black, the colour should always be toned down as has been stressed earlier in preceding chapters and should be really matt.

Engines and Guns

Kit manufacturers and certain reference sources will advise the modeller to paint engines and guns (if fitted) matt black — don't. The colour of engines is a subject in its own right and involves much more than you might reasonably expect and close study of actual powerplants in the Imperial War, RAF and science museums is highly recommended. Exposed cylinders and crankcases can generally be painted with a mix of the main colour. Pushrod covers are aluminium (exposed rods, dull silver) and manifold pipes a dullish copper shade. When the paint has dried the assembly can be further enhanced by carefully applying a thinned dark brown enamel 'wash' overall representing the discharges from the engine. Guns (usually exposed on early warplanes) should be treated to the coat of dark metallic grey obtained by mixing equal proportions of Dark Grey and Aluminium.

Left: a rather unhappy pose for the Linke-Hofmann RI 40/16 reveals the application of standard five colour lozenge fabric. Note that the fabric is also applied over wing struts and wheel covers.

Airscrews

Most of the early aircraft carried large laminated wooden propellors (airscrews) painstakingly carved, then varnished and polished. Where different woods are applicable, these need careful representation by handpainting — there being no other alternative. Sometimes there was brass leading edge sheathing fitted and/or tips covered with fabric and doped in a dull colour. The nuts (or boss if you like) should be a *dull* silver.

Painting

Apart from certain sprayed camouflage patterns on a number of German WW1 aircraft, use of an airbrush is not really necessary for early period aircraft unless they are large flying ones, since most are rather small and masking off would be very complicated indeed. You will find painting biplanes of any period much easier if all colouring and adding of decals is done *before* final assembly takes place.

Wings, fuselage, tail units etc. should be finished completely then assembled together, not forgetting to remove paint from any mating surfaces as otherwise the glue will not adhere properly. An overall finish such as PC10 on RFC aircraft is easily applied and note that often the upper colour 'wrapped around' the lower surface giving an outline appearance when viewed from beneath. Draughting tape can be used to mask off the undersurface colour while the edging is applied. Repair patches and 'newly covered' control surfaces add an extra touch and can be applied by use of a slightly lighter mix of the main colour. The patches can either take the form of a small circle or a square, but do not overdo this.

In most cases of two or multi-colour disruptive patterns such as used by German and French WW1 warplanes, the demarcation lines were hard not

Below: this Dragon Rapide of the Rothman's aerobatic team of 1966 offers an exciting challenge to modellers. The Royal Blue, maroon and white decor will demand careful attention as will the handpainting of the Rothman's crest. The aircraft presents a semi-gloss finish which should reduce even further in small scale.

soft, being applied by brush at the factory and rarely were the colours sprayed on with the exception of certain German two-seaters and bombers.

The various styles of lozenge-painted and pre-coloured fabric of 1914-18 German and Austrian machines are very difficult to apply. SUPERSCALE produce excellent decals of the four-colour German type but you must resort to handpainting the others either by pre-cut stencils with the colours sprayed through or by laboriously tracing the pattern out and handpainting by number.

Aluminium doped finishes often used on early aircraft may cause some problems but if you mix Light Blue (matt) with silver enamel it is easier to apply and certainly more authentic in appearance. In most cases this should be semi-gloss and certainly not too shiny for in general, although most dopes were glossy when new, they toned down considerably during service so that a really shiny finish on such models is to be avoided.

Weathering should be carefully done

This Supermarine Stranraer flying boat has been sprayed with silver paint to which quantities of matt white and light gray have been added to tone down the colour. This offers a fair reproduction of the actual silver dope.

and with reference to photographs wherever possible. Slight exhaust stains over wings or fuselage sides can be applied with Dark Matt Grey, and Dark Brown (suitably thinned) streaked on lower fuselages of rotary engine machines away from the cowling. Mixing up white with Dark Earth, one can apply 'mud' by drybrushing this mix around wheels, tyres, tail skid and perhaps the lower portion of rudders as

well. It could even be extended to wing undersides in line with the wheels where you would expect mud to be thrown up.

Always study photographs of the subject you are modelling whenever you can in order to get the best out of the model and remember to keep colours and varnishes toned down, especially on 1/72nd scale models.

The biggest headache of early civil types such as Dragon Rapides, Moths etc. is the application of the UK 'Block' letter registrations in various colours. Decal manufacturers understandably fail to cater for such subjects but it is surprising how useful WW2 Luftwaffe code letters are as suitable substitutes. Most colours and sizes are available and certainly this is one avenue that should be explored.

C.VII.3540 /16

D1941 /16

235678

Halb C L IV (Rol) 8171/18

The numerals drawn here by the late Peter Gray offer three standard styles of serial application to WW1 German aircraft. The top is for an Albatros CVII, next a typical Albatros fighter, and finally a Roland built Halberstadt CLIV.

Chapter 6

SMALL-SCALE VEHICLES

In general terms, the techniques of painting and finishing small-scale vehicles are just the same as for any other model, but there are some differences in application that should be borne in mind in order to show a small-scale model to its best advantage.

In using the term 'small-scale' we are referring principally to the common scales of 1/72nd and 1/76th. There is a large variety of vehicle kits available in this scale, either intended as accessories to model railways or to complement model aircraft and military dioramas. Generally speaking, the two scales are compatible although it is surprising just how noticeable the difference can be in certain cases. Also relevant within the context of this chapter is the slightly smaller scale of 1/87th, which equates to the continental model railway 'HO' gauge (3mm — 1foot).

'Scale effect' is a phenomenon that is very relevant when modelling vehicles in the smaller scales and this is where the differences of application become apparent. The principal feature that should be treated under the laws of scale effect is the amount of gloss or shine on a model. If you are painting a 1/24th model vehicle with, say a gloss paint, it *can* be applied exactly as it is because the model is large enough to stand the high-gloss finish that results. If, however, you paint a 1/72nd scale vehicle with that same gloss paint the finish will look totally unreal. This is because if your model is 72 times smaller than the

full-size, then so too should the gloss be 72 times less than on the full-size, theoretically.

In practice the treatment is quite simple. It is obviously impractical to reduce the amount of gloss in your tin of paint by such a percentage and the simple answer is to mix gloss *and* matt paints to achieve the correct degree of finish. In general terms a 50-50 mix of matt and gloss will be about right for a 1/72nd model, but it can vary quite a lot according to the actual colour used. It is important, therefore, to practise first by mixing the paint and applying to pieces of scrap plastic card, etc. to determine the correct mix for the colour being applied. A study of the accompanying photographs will show just how much the differences in finish can affect the appearance of a model.

In some cases it will be found that a totally matt finish looks even more appropriate. Military vehicles automatically come into this category because the full-size vehicles are usually matt-finished anyway, but there are some varieties of civilian vehicles that could also be painted matt, or almost matt, in model form. This applies particularly to those vehicles that in full-size form could be said to have had a hard life, for example, coal trucks, earthmoving equipment, etc. These sorts of vehicles are rarely seen 'shiny' and so a matt finish will be more suitable on the model.

As stated, the actual techniques for painting are just the same as for any other model. In other words the model should be properly prepared for

David Jane has used a semi-gloss varnish to obtain the scaled appearance of a gloss finish on this Heller 1/43rd scale Mini.

painting, given at least one undercoat of matt paint, and at least two coats of the final colour. It is vitally important to rub down the paint between coats as this is essential to achieve a nice smooth surface. Use a fine grade wet and dry sandpaper (used wet) for this. Never be tempted to think you can get away with just one coat of paint on a model. You might just get away with it if a good quality matt paint is being used, but certainly not with a gloss paint. The smooth surface of polystyrene might indicate that it is a ready-to-paint surface, but this is not the case, for polystyrene attracts a lot of static and careful preparation is essential to remove this unwelcome attraction. A useful way to show just how static can have an effect is to take a piece of scrap plastic card and give it a coat of gloss paint. Look at it within a couple of minutes and you will see just how much 'muck' has adhered to the paint!

Where metal is the modelling medium, the preparation required is even more important. The soft metal used for most metal kits is a surprisingly absorbent material and the chances of achieving a good finish with just one coat of paint are absolutely *nil*. It is

Left: on larger scale car kits where engine parts are normally moulded in a metallic finish plastic, careful painting using the dry brushing and highlighting techniques will still be necessary.

vitally important to sand all areas of metal kits to be painted, using wet and dry sandpaper and the model *must* then be carefully washed in warm, soapy water to remove all traces of greasiness. From then on, at least two undercoats and two top coats as before.

Up to now we have mentioned the importance of mixing gloss and matt paints to achieve the correct finish for small-scale models. To some degree the minor problems that this entails can be avoided by using certain makes of paint that are now becoming available. For example PRECISION PAINTS

LTD manufacture a range of specially-mixed paints for model railway use, which in most cases is intended to dry to a semi-matt surface. The colours in the range are, of course, matched specifically to railway prototype colours of the various regions, companies etc., but may be used on model vehicles. Another similar product is 'Busmatch' paint, produced by HOWES of Oxford and, as the name implies, these are colours specifically matched to various bus company liveries, and these should also be suitable for general model road vehicle use.

Ted Taylor's C.O.E. White Freightliner with a 6 × 4 tractor unit. Engine powered by Cummings Diesel. An excellent example of an U.S. truck showing a detailed paint scheme with a dusted up exterior.

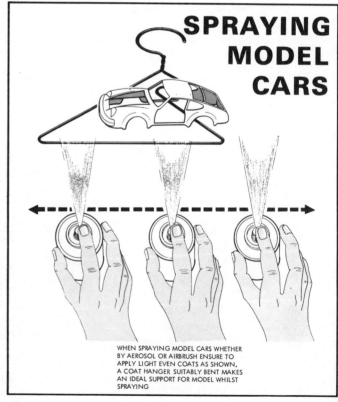

SPRAYING MODEL CARS

WHEN SPRAYING MODEL CARS WHETHER BY AEROSOL OR AIRBRUSH ENSURE TO APPLY LIGHT EVEN COATS AS SHOWN. A COAT HANGER SUITABLY BENT MAKES AN IDEAL SUPPORT FOR MODEL WHILST SPRAYING

The degree of 'scale effect' applied to the major areas of a model road vehicle should also be applied to the minor parts such as tyres, radiators, etc. In large-scale kits the chromed areas are supplied as just that — chromed — and consequently can be fitted to the model without further attention. Chromed parts in small-scale kits are almost unheard of, and this in fact is a good thing. In the same way that a gloss paint looks out of place on a 1/76th model, so too does a chromed surface, being too overpowering in such a small scale. Ordinary silver paint is quite suitable on models in this scale. On metal models, silver paint may be unnecessary. Radiators, bumpers etc. that are meant to be chromed can in fact be polished using an ordinary metal polish. Careful buffing with this will bring up a nice shine that will look just right without being exaggerated.

On a model, scale effect should again play its part and tyres should be painted a suitable dark grey shade, either by mixing black with a small amount of white, or by using a suitable grey paint — HUMBROL Tank Grey is about right. The interiors in most models can be painted in matt colours. In a 1/76th scale model the interior will not be all that visible and so the complications of shine and tone are just not relevant. 'Soft top' areas on models, such as sunshine roofs, can be treated slightly differently. They should be painted in the appropriate matt paint and, when dry, given a coat of matt varnish. This will result in a surface with just the merest hint of a sheen to it that looks just right for the leathercloth type of material often used for this.

It might seem odd that, having spent so much time advising you how to create a perfect finish on your model, we now intend to tell you how to destroy it! Nevertheless that is to an extent the basic theory behind the subject of weathering. This is the term used to cover any form of application on the model intended to represent wear-and-tear, such as dust, mud splashes etc. Of course in most cases the model will be left in 'showroom' condition, but there are occasions when the model can be treated to look like a working vehicle. As an example, supposing a corner of a model railway layout is being modelled to represent, say a quarry. Any showroom condition lorries in such a setting will look most out of place.

There are a number of different ways in which models can be weathered, but as far as small road vehicles are concerned the easiest and most appropriate technique is 'drybrushing' (see Chapter 4).

The same technique can be used for all areas of the model — the underside, for example, will benefit from a bit of drybrushing, using thinned black paint to create a generally oily appearance. A very old and battered vehicle will probably have bare metal showing in places and drybrushing with silver paint will recreate the effect. Practice will show just how useful this technique is, and how much difference it can make to the character of the model in the right circumstances.

Ted Taylor's 1/25th scale Alaskan Hauler has been nicely weathered using an airbrush to 'dust' mud effects around wheels, chassis and lower body sides.

Chapter 7

AFVs — USEFUL TECHNIQUES

Military Modelling magazine has often received numerous requests from readers asking us to elaborate on the whole subject of armour modelling and also give some hints and tips as to how the model can be completed so that it has some individuality but remains within the bounds of scale accuracy. So we decided to take the old TAMIYA Panther V kit as a basis for this.

As with any form of modelling, you must have recourse to reliable reference sources and a glance in the specialist bookshops will give you some idea of the mass of material available. However, as most of us have to work to some sort of budget, we will, where possible, try to utilise the less expensive references, although of course we would make the point that the more books that you can afford, then the wider your scope of reference giving you a greater chance for this apparently elusive individuality. But initially you will find such items as the old BELLONA SERIES of drawings of great help and the AERO PUBLISHERS books or the FIEST PUBLICATIONS are well worth adding to your library. Also we have several inexpensive but well illustrated booklets produced by the Royal Armoured Corps Tank Museum, Bovington Camp, Dorset, who can also supply photographs of most military vehicles and armour, and you should state what type of vehicle you are interested in, what angle(s) you require the photographs to show and so

on; they can also provide scale drawings of much of the combatant's armour and we suggest that you write for their price list, enclosing an SAE.

Before even removing any parts from their sprues it is essential to decide what finish or colour your model is going to be, or, if you start assembly, you will find it well nigh impossible to paint behind the bogies or get at the insides of the main hull, and you can bet some part of the model which you didn't paint will be visible from some angle or another.

We painted the Panther overall in Panzer Grey — which represents the darker shade of grey which was used in the latter years of the war. Having done this, we then carefully painted the simulated rubber tread on each bogey wheel with Humbrol Dunkegrau, which

is sufficiently dark as to look like the wartime German rubber but also contrasts with the basic camouflage finish. Kit instructions often state that bogies, etc., should be painted black, but certainly all that we have seen appear a dark grey colour.

While the bogies are drying, examine the inside of the top hull piece. You will notice that the cooling vents on the rear bodywork may require some slight opening out — this is best done with the tip of a rat tail file. When you are satisfied that the slots etc., are clean, obtain some fine gauze from an old strainer, (we used that from an old coffee strainer — but cheap tea strainers are equally as good). Paint the gauze a deep steel colour.

The headlight is painted to match the

rest of the hull, but with a fine brush paint inside the horizontal slit matt black. When this is dry, carefully paint over this with one single thin coat of gloss varnish to represent the armoured headlight glass.

Our model, for example, is unusual in that only two turret identification numbers appear to have been carried, '65' — normally, three are more common. For example 145 identifies 1st Company (1); 4 indicates the Platoon (4th); and the final numeral is the tank identification or call-number (5). A Tank Commander's vehicle is recognised by the first figure 101,201,301, and those carrying second i/c are number 201,202,203. These numbers appeared in a solid colour red or black with lighter outline when painted against dark surfaces such as white or yellow. The tank number was often repeated on the rear of the turret for identification to following vehicles or infantry, but this was often half the size of that on the sides of the turret.

The German cross appeared in several alternative positions; on the Panther as modelled, they were carried on the sides of the forward hull just above and aft of the first bogie wheel, on left- and right-hand side of the hull. It was also sometimes painted on any flat (or near vertical) area of the rear of the hull however, in all but a very few cases, was very small in size.

The early days of WWII saw advancing German columns with a large red flag upon which appeared a swastika against a white ground, but this was short-lived confidence, particularly when the Allied air offensive increased in 1943/5.

Personal markings on German armour was unusual, but not unknown; this often took the form of a girl's name usually painted in small — 12in. at most — high script on the turret or hull sides.

To return to our model, this bears the 'H' with sword motif of the crack *9th SS Panzer Division Hohenstaufen*, as supplied with the kit, and is placed on the right-hand side of the front glacis plate. The Tamiya kit decals include numeral groupings: 223 and 421 red outlined in white, and 309 in black with white outline, plus four crosses and ten white gun barrel kill rings, together with Divisional markings for 3rd, 1st and 2nd Panzer SS together with other insignia.

COLOURING

A brief summary of armour vehicle camouflage 1941 onwards, would read that in 1941, tanks were either Yellow-Sand and Brown, or Grey and Green for North Africa, and Blue-Grey for other theatres. In 1942, the African scheme was changed to Brown-Sand overall, while a washable white distemper-like paint was introduced for the winter of that year on the Eastern Front. December 18, 1943, saw the old colours ordered to be replaced by Sand-Yellow Primer for *all* fronts, this being a basic factory overall finish. When the new vehicles arrived at their holding units, etc., they were delivered complete with one tin of Olive Drab (which literally matched that used by the Allied armour), a tin of

Weathering enthusiasts can really go to town with military models. Such vehicles rarely look convincing painted in a pristine finish and general dirtying, highlighting, and other effects, as described in this chapter, are well worth considering.

Reddish Brown — what we would call chestnut, and Dark Yellow — which we would refer to as stone. Each colour was packed in a two kilogramme tin and it was left to the discretion of the tank commanders to paint their vehicles 'in the field' to suit local conditions. Many photographs show such paint being applied with a small spraygun — see Fiest's book *Panzerkampfwagen V* for example.

In early spring of 1945 or at about that time, the dark Panzer Grey as matched by Humbrol's paint was introduced for most of the heavy armour, and it is in this final finish that our model was painted.

Lastly we must discuss wear and tear as it affected the finish on these vehicles. Our model was brush-painted (an airbrush finish, unless very well done, provides too good a finish on these larger scale models) as explained in the foregoing text, remembering again to contrast the rubber-covered rim of the bogies.

Before the track was placed over the suspension/bogies, the whole model was lightly brushed with an almost dry brush which had been dipped into Gunmetal and Panzer Grey mixture, then wiped almost dry on a cloth and stippled onto an old newspaper. When the stipple appears almost nothing more than a smudge, you will have obtained the correct load on the brush. This is then very firmly applied over all sharp edges and angular structures to pick out worn metal, etc. — any excess of this can be covered with a similarly near dry application of the basic colour. When this was completed to our satisfaction, we then cut a cheap ¼" wide brush to ¼" length. Similarly, we opened a tin of Matt Earth and USAF Vietnam Tan colour. Pour away the thin liquid, leaving a gooey mess at the bottom of the tin. With the shortened brush, apply this concoction over the wheels, tyres, lower hull etc., until you obtain the right amount of dried-mud-and-dust effect; this will take a little practice, but provided the brush is fairly stiff and the liquid is not liquid but near solid, like heavy porridge, you will soon be applying mud-dried earth stains, etc., with most effective results.

Having completed the muddying to your satisfaction, treat the tracks to the same systematic coverage. But also mix in Dark Earth, Silver, Black, and Red and Black mixed. Use matt colours throughout, of course, for all painting except the Gunmetal colour. When the track has taken on a worn, dirty metallic appearance, position this over the wheels etc.

The Mud...

Finally, to get the dripping/dried mud effect, you again revert to the near-solid Tan and Dark Earth paint and by scraping the edge of the brush over the edges of the hull etc., you find that a 'muddy' build-up occurs very quickly, and when left to dry, hardens very quickly. To represent the dusty scuffing etc., on the upper hull, use a soft brush, dipped into the two mixtures and wiped virtually dry of same again. When applied over the original paint-

work, you will be surprised — and, we hope, pleased — at the way the paint appears like a fine film over everywhere the brush has been.

Don't forget, of course, that all the external stores would be similarly mucky and dusty — but contrasts can be obtained by varying the mixtures or paint used. The groundsheet hanging on the left of the turret is from tissue paper

rolled and bound with model railway lining tape — this is an adhesive tape, coloured, with a one side painted finish. This is best painted over semi-matt Brown or Black to represent leather, or dirty matt Dark Earth to look like webbing, but Germany used more leather than cloth for this type of binding.

Chapter 8

AERO CAMOUFLAGE TECHNIQUES

The basics of painting early period aircraft has already been discussed but later aircraft subjects demand somewhat different methods of approach. The purpose of this short chapter is to discuss some methods of colour application, and no attempt has been made to detail colour schemes, markings, size of national insignia etc., as plenty of reference on these subjects are available elsewhere. We are only concerned here with how the modeller can apply the paints to his model and are assuming he has all the references and correctly mixed colours to hand.

DISRUPTIVE PATTERNS (RAF)

The RAF in WW2 had different camouflage schemes and colours which in general are quite simple to apply either by handpainting or airbrushing. The demarcation lines between colours are important to simulate correctly. Both hard and soft edges can be seen on contemporary photographs. Whether the soft edges can be simulated properly is a matter of debate — the softness is not great and when reduced in scale, actually vanishes. Even the finest airbrush will not give the proper appearance in 1/72nd scale although it may be tolerable in 1/24th or larger.

The pattern should be carefully marked out and the upper surface colours applied first, painting the lighter colour (Dark Earth or one of the Greys)

An example of German Night Fighter camouflage on a Messerschmitt Bf110. Note subtle exhaust stains over wings.

before the Green. Handpainting the pattern is not very difficult on the smaller models but careful reference to the pattern lines is essential. On bigger models, the colours can be sprayed using carefully cut paper stencils to mask off the areas which have to be protected. When that stage is dry, the undersurfaces can be painted, using masking tape to achieve a line between the upper and lower surfaces, if a hard line is required.

Overall finishes such as Trainer Yellow, Night Black or PRU Blue are best airbrushed once you have masked off any transparencies. Exhaust stains

for all types can be applied later, together with such detail as de-icers, walkways, dinghy or gas warning panels, safety markings or special identity bands.

Once the desired markings have been applied, certain other points are worthy of observation, particularly weathering. Bare metal abrasions around canopies, engine and gun panels, foot rests etc. can add a little air of authenticity if carefully represented. Using dull 'silver' thinned down and mixed with matt grey, such paint scrapes can be carefully applied around these areas and on leading edges and propeller blades —

37

but don't overdo it.

When aircraft were re-armed at dispersal, fabric patches were often doped over gun ports in noses or leading edges to prevent any insects or foreign bodies from getting into the gun barrels. Small scraps of decal film can be applied to the model and then painted dull Matt Red — this need not be too neat. Exposed gun barrels were capped by rubber or plastic covers.

A light wash of grey watercolour can accentuate control surfaces if it is applied to the moulded outlines on the kit. These (usually) recessed lines are filled with the paint and then the excess removed with a lint-free cloth. Note this is done *over* the insignia whenever it covers both control and flying surfaces.

SPECIALISED CAMOUFLAGE TECHNIQUES (LUFTWAFFE)

Although the Luftwaffe and Regia Aeronautica used a wide range of colour schemes during the Second World War, the differing applications for the former can be conveniently broken down into three groups. These are splinter, 'RAF type', and blotching, the latter of which appeared as either roughly circular or 'snaking' (mirror wave) and Italian aircraft were commonly mottled in a variety of colours — see Aerocolour tables, Appendix 2.

Splinter camouflage was prevalent on larger German aircraft — the shades varying with aircraft, location and period. The actual division of these colours was an almost hard line on the full-size aircraft that even on a model as large as 1/24th scale is best reproduced

Freehand mottling with an airbrush demands considerable practice.

Above: captured Me262 reveals small mottling along lower fuselage which will be difficult to apply on a 1/72nd model, but feasible on 1/32nd and larger.

as a hard demarcation. Whether you spray or brush by hand, the division lines must be masked to obtain the hard, straight lines desired and *always* start by applying the lighter shades first and ending with the darker, the prime golden rule of painting.

Masking is accomplished with opaque masking tape cut into strips of about ¼" wide as shown in the sketches. After masking the appropriate pattern out, one can fill in the remaining areas not to be painted with Humbrol Maskol or White PVA glue.

The 'RAF type' was a sort of replacement for the splinter camouflage and seen mainly on the wings and spine of Bf109s and Fw190s. The actual division of the colours was a wavy, albeit almost hard line. Application of this finish is rather more tricky unless you own a professional airbrush, the use of which is dealt with in later chapters. For those who own one of the cheaper airbrush/sprayguns, application is not too difficult but use of a mask will still be necessary. The mask is simply a piece of thin card wide enough to cover the wing of the model with a slightly irregular line cut on one edge, and four strips of masking tape about ⅛" from the cut edge. With the spraygun at its smallest setting, hold the mask, tape side down, into the model and spray a

'line' along the edge about ¼" to ¾" wide. Repeat this for the other colour division line, then paint in the remaining middle area. The thickness of the tape ensures the mask does not touch the model surface and a softer line will result after spraying.

With a brush this finish is very difficult to achieve but a compromise would be to paint the appropriate area in with hard divisional lines. Then with a 50-50 mix of the two colours involved, paint a thin line using an 0 or 00 brush along the hard edge which will slightly soften the colours together.

Finally we come to the blotching and mottling effects in its many forms which was applied to the fuselage sides on fighters and upper surfaces of night-fighters. Again you should have no problem if you own a professional airbrush and even with the cheaper ones, on larger scale models at least, a good representative finish can still be obtained. For applying smallish mottling or 'snaking' on smaller models, again a mask will have to be used. The mask is in the form of piece(s) of card with small holes, about two thirds the size roughly of the size blotchings that are required. This is then held just off the surface of the model and the paint sprayed through the holes — the softness of the mottle depends on how far

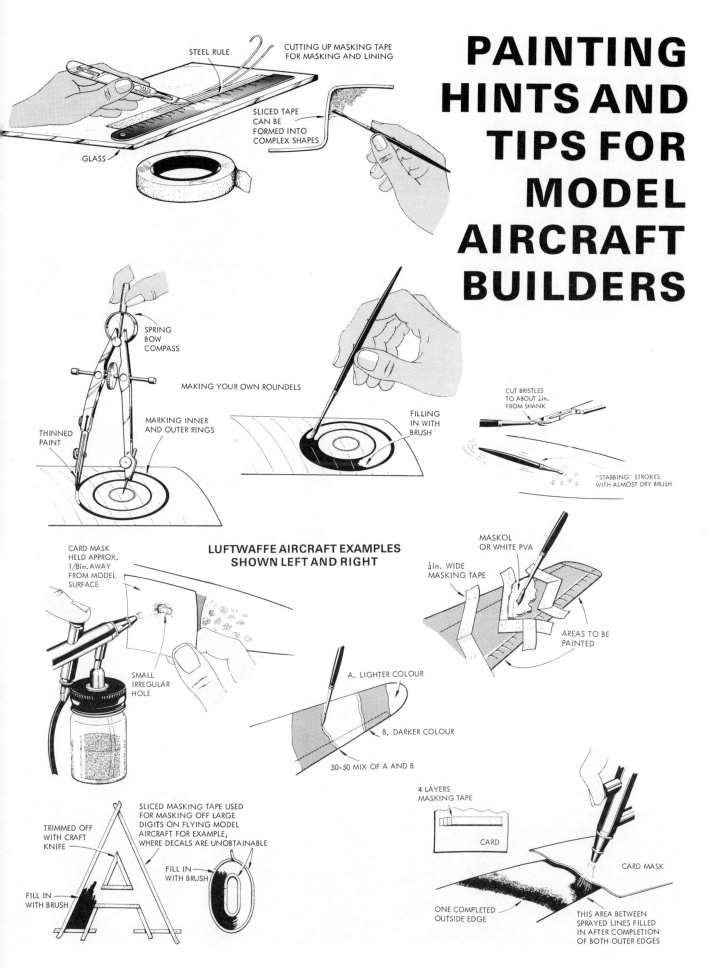

PAINTING HINTS AND TIPS FOR MODEL AIRCRAFT BUILDERS

STEEL RULE

CUTTING UP MASKING TAPE
FOR MASKING AND LINING

GLASS

SLICED TAPE
CAN BE
FORMED INTO
COMPLEX SHAPES

SPRING
BOW
COMPASS

MAKING YOUR OWN ROUNDELS

THINNED
PAINT

MARKING INNER
AND OUTER RINGS

FILLING
IN WITH
BRUSH

CUT BRISTLES
TO ABOUT ⅛in.
FROM SHANK

"STABBING" STROKES
WITH ALMOST DRY BRUSH

CARD MASK
HELD APPROX.
1/8in. AWAY
FROM MODEL
SURFACE

**LUFTWAFFE AIRCRAFT EXAMPLES
SHOWN LEFT AND RIGHT**

MASKOL
OR WHITE PVA

¼in. WIDE
MASKING TAPE

AREAS TO BE
PAINTED

SMALL
IRREGULAR
HOLE

A. LIGHTER COLOUR

B. DARKER COLOUR

50–50 MIX OF A AND B

TRIMMED OFF
WITH CRAFT
KNIFE

SLICED MASKING TAPE USED
FOR MASKING OFF LARGE
DIGITS ON FLYING MODEL
AIRCRAFT FOR EXAMPLE,
WHERE DECALS ARE UNOBTAINABLE

FILL IN
WITH BRUSH

FILL IN
WITH BRUSH

4 LAYERS
MASKING TAPE

CARD

CARD MASK

ONE COMPLETED
OUTSIDE EDGE

THIS AREA BETWEEN
SPRAYED LINES FILLED
IN AFTER COMPLETION
OF BOTH OUTER EDGES

39

away from the model the mask is held. Mirror wave demands good control of the brush by setting it fine and running around the model surfaces holding it about ½″ away from the surface. This technique demands a great deal of practice to master.

With a brush the mottling effects are best achieved using a cropped, fairly good quality brush (leaving about ¼″ of bristle) which is then dipped in the paint, wiped almost clean then stippled with stabbing strokes onto the model. It hardly needs stressing that the mottle and RAF type finishes whether applied by spraygun or brush really need to be *practised*, preferably on an old model or scrap card before attempting it on your definitive model creation.

The completed model can then be varnished to hold down the decals and provide a neat overall appearance and this is best done before weathering takes place. Never use pure matt or pure gloss but tone these down for the appropriate finish desired, again studying references.

The notes, although concentrating mainly on RAF and Luftwaffe techniques, can be applied to most aircraft from WW2 period onwards. The modern camouflages on NATO and USAF aircraft can be applied in much the same way, depending on their particular styles. Either gloss, matt and satin finishes can be seen on current aircraft and again study of photos will show the kind of result you need to aim at.

Right, Hotspur glider shows hard and soft demarcation lines and weathered fabric painted finish. Note that the black bands applied over the Trainer Yellow undersides have been roughly applied, however this is not an excuse for a slapdash approach by the modeller for a slightly wavy line on a full-size aircraft will disappear when produced on a 1/72nd scale model — so always use masking tape.

Compare weathered appearance of this Typhoon with the pristine Spitfire Mark XIV shown below. Even so the colours on the latter do not appear to have covered very well as can be seen on the patchy Dark Green areas of the camouflage.

Remember that varnishes tend to darken colours so a little matt white mixed in the enamels beforehand may help to retain correct shades.

Chapter 9

PAINTING MODEL SHIPS

STEAM

Ideally, scale models require scale paint, but of course as previously discussed this particular ideal is rather difficult and so some compromise has to be accepted. The smaller the scale of the model, the greater has to be the compromise, and the warship modeller just has to recognise this fact. There are various ways in which the problem can be alleviated, however, and these will be outlined later. On the other hand, the warship modeller will only infrequently be called upon to simulate a natural metal finish, search for authentic interior colour schemes or deftly apply decals (all of which cause headaches at some time or another for those whose bent is miniature aircraft or vehicles), and hardly ever will he be required to produce a flawless gloss finish. The

larger the scale of his subject, of course, the more likely will he need to employ these skills, but, generally speaking, his approach can be described as the careful application of sombre hues and the delicate portrayal of effects that cannot be reproduced merely by using a few brushfuls of paint straight out of the tin.

Because of the size and consequent intricacy of small-scale warship models, it is doubtful whether an airbrush offers much advantage over the time-honoured — and of late much maligned — paint brush when it comes to applying the colours. Rarely is an immaculate finish required, *never* an overspray effect, and further, the work involved in preparatory masking is hardly worth the effort when one considers the results achieved. For larger scale subjects, 1/72nd for

example, the airbrush will certainly be of value, for the same reasons that it is of value to the aircraft modeller. Worthy of more attention is the consistency of the paint that is used. As supplied by the manufacturers, it is simply far too thick for a realistic finish, and should be reduced to something approaching the density of water by diluting it drastically with thinners or white spirit. This process also has the incidental but valuable advantage of toning down the strength of the colours, more of which to follow.

The method followed for painting a model warship will to some extent depend upon the preferences of the individual modeller, but in some respects it differs from that required for other types of model. First of all, life is made

Below left, 1/700th scale *HMS Prince of Wales* painstakingly painted in RN camouflage pattern, model at right is to larger 1/400th scale — The Prinz Eugen from Heller. Note subtle downward streaks on the hull of latter.

very difficult if the subject is assembled in its entirety before any painting is started. A far neater result will generally be achieved if a stage-by-stage approach is adopted, with each sub-assembly, or in some instances individual part, painted *before* it is added to the model. Another general recommendation is that horizontal surfaces be painted before vertical surfaces wherever possible.

Methods

As with all plastic modelling, careful preparation of the kit components is essential. Small scales demand that greater attention be paid to moulding flaws, the removal of dust etc., than is perhaps otherwise necessary. Relatively little filling should be required, but even tiny gaps should not go unheeded, and these can be dealt with by allowing gloss paint to run along them, any excess being wiped off using a rag dampened with white spirit. Areas which have been filled with one of the proprietary compounds should be 'primed' either with liquid cement or with very thin matt paint. Undercoating is not usually necessary, except where a natural light wood finish is to be applied, and here, once again, extra thin matt white paint does the job satisfactorily.

After the initial preparation, the first stage in painting a ship model is usually the application of colour to the weatherdecks. A good quality soft brush of medium size should be used, the paint should be worked thoroughly into the angles made by any moulded hatches, ventilators, etc., and the final strokes should be made longitudinally. In fact it's a good idea to work from the stern forward, moving along the decks about an inch or so at a time, brushing towards the stern. If planked surfaces are to be represented, any slight variations in tone caused by the paint not covering entirely evenly can be ignored, unless a pristine 'Fleet Review' finish is called for. For steel-plated or linoleum-covered decks etc., extra care is required to ensure that evenness of finish is achieved. This can be accomplished by working quickly, trying to complete the painting of the last area before the

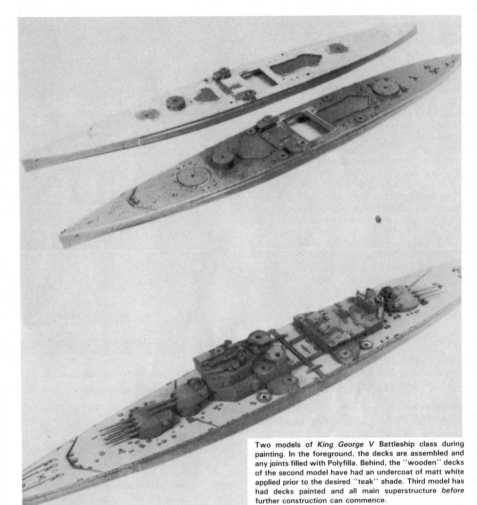

Two models of *King George V* Battleship class during painting. In the foreground, the decks are assembled and any joints filled with Polyfilla. Behind, the "wooden" decks of the second model have had an undercoat of matt white applied prior to the desired "teak" shade. Third model has had decks painted and all main superstructure *before* further construction can commence.

first has dried. For large-area decks this is not always possible, and the overlaps can be so arranged that they are unseen on the completed model, for example by hiding them between boat crutches.

What is perhaps the most difficult part of painting a ship model is tackled next — the multitude of hatches, vents, windlasses, chafing plates, protective plating, and all the other moulded detail which, if not neatly picked out, can ruin the appearance of an otherwise good model. It is perfectly possible to paint the vertical surfaces of this raised detail provided a pointed brush is used — not necessarily of a small size — very lightly loaded with thinned paint. Care

Below, 1/700th scale, *HMS Nelson* ploughs through a "Polyfilla" sea. In this case the paint scheme is very simple but even so still demands care and patience in application.

should be exercised to ensure that no paint strays onto the surrounding decking — better to finish a little too high than to allow the paint to flood into the corners.

The major vertical surfaces of the model, i.e. the hull and superstructure, comprise the next principal stage. First, all recessed detail such as scuttles should be painted blackish grey, with any excess removed with a rag. Where scuttles are represented by raised circles, it is worthwhile opening them up with a drill as this eases considerably the job of painting the adjacent areas.

It is a great temptation to run the brush along the length of the hull, but this should be resisted as a more realistic effect can be obtained by using vertical strokes. A flattish brush, again lightly loaded, will ensure that no paint runs into the recessed scuttles. Any brush marks that may be left can be turned to advantage (in fact they can be deliberately induced) to represent the streaking, downwash, etc., that are inevitable features of ships in service. When the hull is completely dry, the boot topping area can be masked off and painted. Strips of Sellotape ⅛″ wide or less will permit a certain amount of stretching to take in the contours of the bows and stern. The superstructure should also be painted in vertical strokes, though for obvious reasons any streaking should be less pronounced.

The smaller fittings — masts, rangefinders, boats, armament (if fitted) and so forth — should all be painted before they are added to the model, and the techniques already mentioned apply here also. 'Shadow shading' may be usefully applied to such things as solid boat decking, lattice work and funnel interiors.

Effects

The application of camouflage warrants one or two special considerations. As 'watery' paint is to be used, it is essential that any colours previously applied be left to dry out thoroughly, preferably over forty-eight hours, and efforts should be made to ensure that as little overlap of colours as possible

Prinz Eugen to 1/400th scale shows typical German camouflage of light and dark grey, designed to "foreshorten" the length of the ship.

occurs. Demarcation lines can be carefully drawn out using a fine brush, with infilling being completed as rapidly as possible, again with vertical brush strokes. Camouflaged upperworks present peculiar problems: it is easier to apply the paint before the various structures are fixed in position, but this means that demarcation lines have to be painted in with the structures dry fitted to make certain they match up.

It may not always be possible to use scale paint on scale models, but one can go some way towards achieving scale colour and scale lustre, and in a way the techniques required here may be likened to producing a three-dimensional painting. Thinning the paint helps considerably, as previously noted; greater effect can be obtained by reducing the intensity of the colours and reducing their purity (especially with regard to black and white) by careful preparation of the paint mixes. On the rare occasions when a glossy finish would need to be simulated (Sea Blue Gloss US Navy carrier aircraft spring to mind), the lustre should also be lessened, for example by adding an appropriate amount of flatting agent. In almost all circumstances the exterior surfaces of a model warship should carry a completely flat finish — almost all but not

quite. The writer was once severely chastised for producing a model on which the forecastle deck featured a restrained semi-gloss sheen. The fact that the subject was depicted at a simulated 30 knots and well and truly 'taking it green' seemed to have escaped the critic's attention!

Weathering effects on small-scale warships should at all times be tackled with extreme caution as regards both the strength of the shades used and the extent to which they are applied. The hull of course, especially the bows, is the area most prone to paint erosion, but the colour contrasts should be gentle, and greys will suffice for most requirements. Drybrushed rust may be touched in below the hawsepipes, but one should be very wary of using this particular colour anywhere else. Other wear and tear techniques have already been briefly described.

A final word — the greater the acquaintance you have with the full-scale subject, the more 'feel' you acquire for it, and it should follow that your model will be more realistic. There is no substitute for the real thing, but the next best is a set of good photographs. This will be obvious to most, but it is surprising how many still appear not to appreciate the fact.

SAIL

The following methods were those used when building the AIRFIX *Discovery*, a kit which is very finely detailed and well worth taking pains to finish to exhibition standard. The deck-houses in particular, lend themselves to fine painting, for while they are full of detail, that detail is not exaggerated. There is no built-in wood texture, which is an intelligent omission, since examination of the ship's models in museums will reveal that wood texture appears only as colour variation. The imitation of woodgrain is no help at all to modellers going for accurate scale effect in ships. Effort wasted in this way would be better employed in the production of useful detail, such as jack-stays and stanchions on yards, which are moulded into the *Discovery* yards. We have made mention of this as an example of what to look for when selecting a kit.

With the exception of Matt Khaki and Matt White no plastic enamels were used; instead colours were selected from various types of artists' gouache. Here is a list from which to make a selection to suit various requirements for finish.

Daler-Rowney Cryla Colour
(Waterproof, very smooth, non-gloss)

Yellow Ochre
Golden Ochre
Cadmium Orange
Raw Umber
Burnt Umber
Burnt Sienna
Venetian Red

Beautifully built and painted is the much modified Airfix *Discovery* built by Tony Buckley of IPMS. In this instance extensive use of waterproof Cryla colours were used in preference to enamels.

Daler-Rowney Acrylic Designers' Gouache
(Waterproof, matt)

In addition to the above colours select Black and White and Vandyke Brown from this range.

Pelikan Plaka
(Waterproof poster paint)

Yellow Ochre
Yellow Brown
Yellow
Orange
Brown
Red-Brown
White
Black

Daler-Rowney Professional Designers' Gouache
(Non-waterproof)

The colours listed so far should be sufficient for most requirements but they can be supplemented by selections made from this range. These paints are not waterproof but can be easily fixed and made fast by varnishing with various Daler-Rowney products, details of

Fishing trawler Sheila by Charles Somerville is modelled from plans published in Radio Control Boat Modeller magazine.

which are given in the artists' materials catalogue, or by coating with plastic model varnish.

The technique employed is straightforward requiring only care and patience, plus a selection of good quality sable hair brushes for *oil* painting, Numbers 00 to 4. Care should be taken that the waterproof colours do not dry on the brushes.

Painting the Deck

Paint the deck over with Matt Khaki, Matt White or a mixture of both, carefully leaving unpainted those areas to which deck-houses, bollards etc., are to be glued later. Allow to dry thoroughly. With a very fine needle and a steel ruler scribe through the paint to the plastic lightly, carefully delineating each plank of the deck.

The basic deck colour is then mixed in a palette. This is largely a matter for the individual modeller to decide for himself. However, the decks are a very pale oak, bleached by stoning and saltwater. The colour is made from Yellow Brown tinting White in Plaka. This is painted over the deck, allowed to dry and followed by the scribing process again. The mixture in the palette is then altered slightly, with a touch of Orange added. Select a few planks at random and colour over with a dilute solution of this colour, and again alter the mixture

by making it slightly darker with the addition of a very small amount of Burnt Umber. Again select a few planks in a random fashion and colour over, brushing fore and aft. Occasionally two planks of the same colour lie side by side or both together. This process continues until the deck looks just right. Do not try to do too much mixing with the same palette of colour, since after a time no variation is possible and the colour will have dulled beyond usefulness, but rather mix up a fresh palette of the same basic variations. When the colouring is completed apply the scribing process once again. Just for the sake of extra safety, we varnished the deck with Daler-Rowney Matt varnish. This finish looks right from a distance and stands up to close examination.

The same techniques can be applied to the bare oak hulls of period ships. It is more difficult to scribe the curves of a hull, but once this has been done the needle follows the original groove easily if very slight pressure is applied. The ship's boats are treated in the same way. The deck-houses also are given the same treatment, together with the paddles of the ship's boats. The deck-houses are a darker wood (Yellow Brown darkened with Brown), and variations of this, with an application of 50 per cent gloss/50 per cent matt Airfix varnish. Portholes are picked out in off-white, and at this scale, the windows represented by

Black Plaka.

The masts, yards and bowsprit of *Discovery* are painted in Daler-Rowney Cryla paint. The oak mast represented by an application of translucent white over Burnt Umber, followed by a coat of dilute Golden Ochre. The same treatment is given to the yards and bowsprit, the yard tips being white. The decking of the crows' feet is brought out in the same way as the main deck, though using slightly darker shades. The darker woods of cross-trees, trestle-trees, checks etc., are again well defined by, for example, having a slight difference in colour between cross-trees and trestle-trees.

The hull below the water line is given two coats of Black Plaka over a Khaki undercoat, then Matt varnished, with the wale and topgallant-rail picked out in Red-Brown Plaka and semi-gloss varnish.

The Plimsoll line in this case was one long piece of very thin stretched white sprue held on the hull with very carefully applied liquid polystyrene cement applied after painting. We do not necessarily recommend this as it can, if mishandled, ruin a good paint job, and white lines of suitable width are available in Letraset anyway.

Below, *Royal Louis*, a much modified Heller kit pictured during construction and painted with acrylics. Note variations of colour in deck planking.

CUSTOM SPRAYING – THE TECHNIQUES EXPLAINED

Having worked mainly on very small-scale cars and vans, I soon realised that some of the larger scales such as the 1/8th models available from, say, Monogram would provide an excellent platform for a really special out-of-the-rut paint job which would do the model justice. I also decided that metalflake paints could be used as an exercise in

really special custom spraying. Before starting the model, a trip to the local art centre yielded various materials with which I could weigh up preliminary drawing designs for the murals and the spray job destined for the car; and also to finalise the colours to use for a really flashy paint job.

For the purpose of these 'roughs',

inks for spraying onto cartridge paper were used which are very thin and allow finer lines to be achieved (this is also a good way of practising your airbrushing!). Modellers often ask about paint consistencies, and the surprising answer is not the usual one of 50-50 paint and thinners, but 60% thinners to 40% paint. Occasionally 70% thinners to 30% paint can be used or even at one extreme 90% to 10% paint. This system also applies to watercolours, enamels, cellulose and acrylic paints, but when using these widely spaced proportions, spray *thin* coats, *making sure each coat is dry* before applying another. It obviously takes longer and you may need as many as five or six coats, but the result is worth the effort, as one or two thick coats can easily obliterate panel lines, rivets, vents and other types of surface detail and ruin the desired effect.

After the ideas for the drawings and colours were roughed out and decided, another trip was made to the local auto spray shop, ultimately leaving there with the necessary tinned paints and flake with which to start. Later, work was started on the actual kit. Although the 1932 Ford Roadster is no longer listed in the Monogram list, there are other large-scale models just as interesting. Being a collector of kits I was working from a model stored in my loft for a long time!

The engine and gearbox were airbrushed with Metalflake Candy Apple Gold Ground Coat, all the chrome parts (except the chromed carburettors) were assembled and then brush painted with silver to give a more realistic effect. When the engine was wired up, the fuel lines fitted, and everything else looked satisfactory, work commenced on the chassis, which was left black. Next to assemble were steering, prop shaft, back axle, brake drums and the petrol tank parts which were also left in the natural black plastic. The raised letters on the tyres were painted with white watercolour acrylics, after the wheels were fitted, and then the engine and gearbox were dropped in.

Now came the moment to commence proper airbrushing, so out came the roughs drawn previously, together with the necessary colours. Before mixing the colours, one door of the model was opened up in the bodywork and the bonnet also cut into open position, later these were taped back into place ready for spraying. Using the colour and

thinners in the ratio of 70% thinners 30% paint, the entire car body, wings and bonnet were sprayed in Gold Ground Coat, the first two coats being *misted* on from a distance of about a foot or so as to dry quickly before getting the chance to attack the plastic and as this paint *does* dry quickly, these coats can be applied rapidly. It is worth pointing out that this paint gives off a very heavy vapour and so it is vital to spray in a well ventilated area, i.e. the back garden, or at the very least wear a face mask.

When dry, I then oversprayed the base colour in Candy Apple Tangerine (two coats) and allowed the model to dry thoroughly. It wasn't necessary to use a top line airbrush as the area here is quite large. In fact a Badger 200 can be opened up to cover these areas. It was subsequently loaded with Red Candy and adjusted to fine, in order to

undertake the freehand 'fogging', which is where Candy Apple or 'Candies' really come into their own for such subtle colour changes, (see Fig. 1).

While this red was drying the next step was to mix up Burnt Orange, a little red and a touch of black, adding to the cup and adjusting the brush to a mere pencil line and spraying around the body panels freehand (Fig. 2). After this was done, the body was put to one side and the process repeated on the wings. Then the mirror-flake particles available, were mixed in small clear tubes with clear acrylic lacquer using a larger airbrush (the 350) for applying the mirror-flake. If the latter appears to be too heavy (although three grades are available), for scale it can be ground finer with pestle and mortar. A Badger 250 could have been used but this would have created an all-over effect and the requirement is for a more concentrated effect i.e. around the edges of the wheel arches and wings to give a fogged or shadow effect. (Fig. 3.)

Both Badger 350 and 250 brushes are able to cope with metalflake particles suspended in lacquer but practice is needed as this is a very different medium to use and needs time to get right. Once the mirror-flake was applied the edges were again oversprayed with Red Candy, after which the entire body, wings and bonnet were given at least 20 coats of clear lacquer thinned down to 60% − 40% in order to seal in the flake for a smooth overall finish.

All the foregoing appears to be a

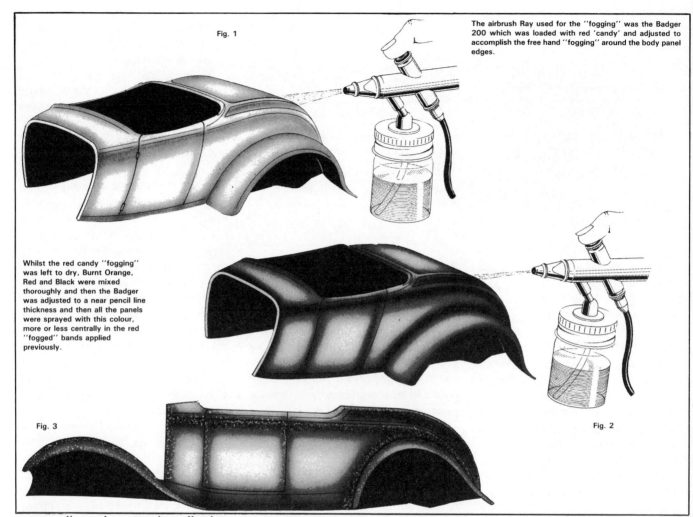

Fig. 1

The airbrush Ray used for the "fogging" was the Badger 200 which was loaded with red 'candy' and adjusted to accomplish the free hand "fogging" around the body panel edges.

Whilst the red candy "fogging" was left to dry, Burnt Orange, Red and Black were mixed thoroughly and then the Badger was adjusted to a near pencil line thickness and then all the panels were sprayed with this colour, more or less centrally in the red "fogged" bands applied previously.

Fig. 3

Fig. 2

never ending task — spraying, allowing to dry and respraying — but in not rushing you can achieve a really fine result. If you *do* rush the job and do not allow the many coats to dry properly, the top coat dries but the inner coats shrink as they dry and cause the top to crack.

Next stage was to spray the seats and panelling free-hand with Candies, toning to suit the appearance of the body, the effect being visible in our photographs.

The masking up of the various murals adorning the side panels was the next step. A low tack clear masking film was used such as that marketed by Badger, Revell etc., and a sharp scalpel to cut it. All the background work was freehand airbrushing, and this needed a really good quality double action airbrush. I used a Badger 100 with the finest needle and nozzle, but any of the top quality alternatives would do.

Finally, a coat of clear lacquer was

Ray Habgood even airbrushed the seats for added effect on the Monogram Street Rod by carefully "fogging" around the moulded detail. Be prepared for spending a little time on lacquering, smoothing and polishing when producing the exterior finish.

sprayed on to seal it all in. Then the murals were re-masked and the hot-rod car designs were drawn on the film using a sharpened Chinagraph pencil; then the appropriate areas were cut out with the scalpel and sprayed freehand. The doors were then lined in, the masking removed and the fineline airbrushing carried on with until completed. If desired an ordinary brush can be used for hard-line highlights. To finish this stage, the murals were given two spray coats of clear lacquer to seal, and then the entire paint job rubbed down with 1200 wet and dry. For the grand finale, four fine coats of 90% − 10% thinners and lacquer were sprayed to achieve a glass-like finish and give the mirror-flake a real 3-D appearance.

You should know that *Metalflake* is the trade name for an American Company specialising in custom finishes for full-size car enthusiasts. They are available in the UK from various specialist firms a few of which used to provide small decanted tins of all the colours mentioned in this chapter, plus a vast range of others, not to mention masking materials, thinners, airbrushes, colour charts, etc.

One of the major problems with products such as Metalflake, is that it is packaged in the sort of quantities suited for custom painting the 'real thing' and this does tend to be a bit over the top for the miniature customiser. Working with others of similar interest helps, for it enables large cans of any given colour to be shared out evenly amongst the group. An alternative might well be to try to make contact with a local garage that specialises in custom paint jobs and do a deal with the paint shop foreman. In many cases, you can get the odd eggcup-full of paint that you need, from their stock, for the price of a few beers.

Car customising is not quite the industry it was a year or so ago, but careful scrutiny of the *Yellow Pages* might well find a custom service near you.

Metalflake brand of paints (including the Candies, flakes and the exotic-like flip-flop and eerydess) is imported to the U.K. by: Metalflake U.K., 25, Tulworth Park Road, Tulworth, Surrey KT6 7RN. Tel. 081-390-6844.

Another view of Ray Habgood's Monogram Street Rod.

Chapter 11

DECALS — A GUIDE TO CARE AND APPLICATION

The vast amount of commercial decal (transfer) sheets available to aircraft, armour and auto modellers is seemingly endless with new releases appearing almost weekly. Therefore it may be presumed that a few notes in aiding modellers to get the best from decals, whether they be from the kit or produced in their own right, may be useful. The once accepted principle of dipping transfers in a saucer of water and simply sliding off their backing sheets onto the model surface has long since been superseded by more elaborate methods.

The main exponent of these methods is Super Scale of the USA whose *Super Scale System* has endeared them to many modellers and we will describe the

process in depth once we have dealt with some preliminary advice on the application of 'standard' decals. Incidentally the methods prescribed for the Super Scale System can be used on most other brands of decals always assuming

they are not too thick. The exception, of course, are the pressure-sensitive type produced by Letraset and others which do not require soaking.

Although these days most kits contain high quality decal sheets, do not expect them all to match the high standards set by Modeldecal, Rareliners, ATP and Super Scale — because many of them will not. Indeed there are several leading kit manufacturers whose decals leave a great deal to be desired; but with such extensive ranges available to the enthusiast there is now little excuse for any model to be poorly decorated.

Most serious modellers will probably build up a 'decal bank' because as more and more kits supply alternative decals, a surprising number can be collected over a period of time and of course as commercial sheets often provide several choices, there are even more leftovers. Decal sheets need to be carefully stored (boxed) in polythene sleeves and most

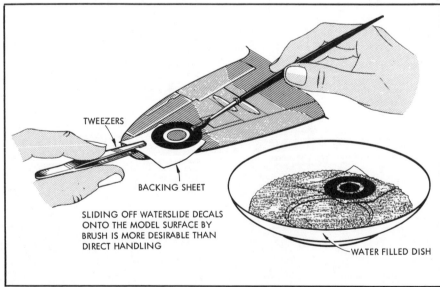

TWEEZERS

BACKING SHEET

SLIDING OFF WATERSLIDE DECALS ONTO THE MODEL SURFACE BY BRUSH IS MORE DESIRABLE THAN DIRECT HANDLING

WATER FILLED DISH

important, kept away from damp or strong heat and light sources. An old shoe box would be an ideal container.

World War Two and later, remain the most popular periods throughout the majority of commercial decal ranges, with current airliners fast becoming a close second. WWI decals are comparatively rare (strange when this period saw some of history's most gaily coloured aircraft) and the poor between-wars enthusiast has even less to crow about . . .

APPLICATION

The workbench should be cleared of *all* painting materials, glue and irrelevant tools and a few items of specialised equipment gathered together. A soft lint-free cloth is a first essential together with a dish of tepid water, a pair of *sharp* scissors, a craft knife, tweezers and a small sable brush. If using the Super Scale System there are additional materials in the form of Extra Gloss varnish and two fixing liquids.

Most waterslide decals are based on a carrier film which you must endeavour to render invisible at all costs. Trimming the excess away with scissors is a logical remedy, but can often prove difficult to those without a steady hand and especially when it comes to cutting round very small emblems or digits.

Additionally, for any decal to adhere firmly upon the model surface, the finish of the model should be gloss, not matt. A matt finish is quite rough causing minute 'pockets' of air to be trapped in the surface irregularities and so it prevents the decal from seating firmly therefore adhesion will suffer as a result.

Assuming that you have a gloss finished model to hand, the decals are prepared by immersing the subjects one by one into the water for a few seconds and then quickly removing. They can be slid off the backing paper with the sable brush, but at all costs try to avoid handling the decals directly as some can quite easily be damaged. Once satisfied that the subject is in the correct position, gently press with the cloth to remove any excess moisture. Each decal should

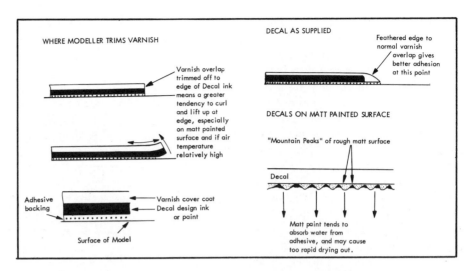

be applied individually and the operation should not be rushed — also the model should be carefully handled as it is all too easy to accidentally remove a recently applied decal.

The brush and the tweezers will be found very useful in nudging decals into place, especially when very small 1/72nd stencils are to be used. After the decals have been left for 24 hours to dry out, any extensive carrier film still present can be carefully cut away using the craft knife. After this, the model can now be varnished in the appropriate sheens and the two coats of varnish, before and after decal application, should ensure the disappearance of any carrier film untrimmed.

PRESSURE-SENSITIVE DECALS

At one time, it looked as though the 'rub-down', Letraset style of decal would completely eclipse the old-fashioned waterslide but, in practice, this did not happen.

Letraset themselves produced a range of dry-print decals covering most of the major combatants of WW2. Alas these are no longer available. Rub-down decals do exist in other areas of scale modelling and there are examples of the highest quality available to the model railway enthusiast.

Letraset (and other equivalent brands like Meccanorma and Alfac) concentrated mainly on the high turnover end of their business and the graphics and printing industry has come to rely heavily on these products.

While RAF roundels and German crosses may no longer be available, a lot of 'standard' lettering can be pressed into service on scale models and the wide-awake modeller will capitalise on the differences between this style of product and the waterslide. The new decals arrive on a semi-opaque carrier and are held *beneath* it rather than over it, a waxed backing sheet protects the adhesive side. To apply, the subject is held over the correct position and the top of the sheet burnished with a special Letraset tool until the subject is transferred to the model. Later more burnishing can take place using the backing paper over the decal so as not to tear it. The technique takes practice and has one distinct disadvantage in that once positioned and burnishing commences there is no way of altering the decal's

Below: Revell's 1/72nd Fokker DVII has been entirely clad with Superscale decals following techniques as described on pages 52 and 53. Careful preparation being vital before cutting up the decal sheets. (The 'Superscale System' can also be used with most other brands of decal). The lozenge pattern shown here is a good representation of the four colour pattern, further details of which are found in the WW1 Aero Colour table. Overall finish of this model is semi-gloss using Ronseal Polyurethane.

position. If incorrectly positioned initially, it has to be removed with Sello-tape and replaced — in this respect pressure-sensitive types can be wasteful.

If carefully applied however, their distinct advantages are considerable. There is no carrier film, there is no real problem of covering compound areas, there is no need for water, liquid, brushes etc., and the finished result is most convincing. Difficulty might occur while lining up the decal's position on the model, and it might be helpful if part of the carrier holding the decal is removed and taped to the model with masking tape while burnishing takes place. The decals must be burnished down with care, too vigorous an action and stretching and distortion will occur and slight splitting is possible. Always keep the backing paper beneath the sheet to prevent dust or scraps adhering to the adhesive face of the sheet which will result in bumps appearing under the decals when next applied. Store in a dustfree box as you would any other kind of decal and certainly do not expose them to strong sunlight.

Pressure-sensitive decals really score when there are small stencils or numerals to be added, and of course commercial artist Letraset sheets can provide many of these. In fact the Patent Specification at the foot of each sheet will yield a great number of miniscule letters and numerals. The wide range of letter and number styles and the wide choice of brands, offers the modellers untold combinations — most often in black, although many styles are available in white and just a few in a limited range of colours. Even foreign languages are available for those modelling, say, Middle Eastern vehicles. Few of the wide range of letter styles, though, really fall into our catchment area and sans serif letter styles are likely to be of most use. Flying scale modellers have already discovered that Letraset stencil styles are of great use for markings on R/C and C/L models.

Some manufacturers actually started to include pressure decals within their kit boxes but surprisingly the idea did not appear to really catch on. Although remaining a minority in the decal world, it is surprising that the advantages of pressure-sensitive types have not per-suaded more manufacturers to produce them.

Letraset sheets will provide a range of items to decorate most models, and the standard range of numerals and letters will offer even more but they will not always come in required colours. Black or white is usually the only choice. There are however, ways to overcome this.

Suppose silver digits are required to be painted on a red background, (i.e. for a pre-War Tiger Moth) and the only letters obtainable in the correct style were in black. Find a spare piece of decal carrier film and paint it silver, leaving to dry for at least 24 hours. Then apply the desired serial, registration etc. in black Letraset and thinly overpaint the whole lot in red. (The second colour is best sprayed over silver, as brushing can soften it, but is otherwise satisfactory for other colours.) When dry, tack some self-adhesive tape onto the painted area, press gently on the letter and then peel off. The black Letraset which has now done its job should carefully lift away, attached to the Sellotape and it leaves silver letters standing through from the first coat with a a red surround. This simple use of Letraset to stencil a reverse colour application has now made a waterslide transfer which can then be trimmed and then applied as a normal decal to a red-painted fuselage or body shell. On bigger models the process could be applied directly to the model but the transfer allows for easier positioning. For the really dedicated modeller, specialist supplies can, and will, produce single sheets of rub-down decals to order — expensive but so accurate, and sometimes well worth the cost.

THE SUPER SCALE SYSTEM EXPLAINED

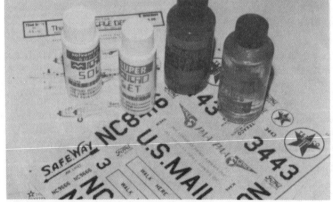

(1) The Super Scale System lines up: from left to right, Super-sol (Red Label) decal softener, Superset (Blue Label) wetting agent, Extra Flat and Extra Gloss — both varnishes. The bottles are all plastic and if carefully capped should not deteriorate. *You must avoid breathing the vapours of either at all costs.*

(2) Before Super Scale (or any other brand of) decals are applied, the model must be gloss varnished irrespective of its intended finish. Always leave windows open and always wear a mask when spraying the Extra gloss — we make no excuse for belabouring this point. Apply two fine coats and leave model to dry thoroughly. (Working with Extra colour gloss paints will alleviate this stage!)

(3) Carefully cut out each design — close trimming is not essential — dip into lukewarm water. Do not oversoak otherwise this will tend to seriously affect the adhesive qualities of the decal.

(4) About 60 seconds should be sufficient time immersed in water for a Super Scale decal. When items are rather small the use of tweezers is to be recommended, but take care to grip the backing sheet wherever possible — not the decal itself as here!

(5) While the decal is softening, unscrew the Superset bottle and brush onto the appropriate model surface. Almost any medium (soft) sable brush will do. Superset contains a wetting agent and its purpose is to eliminate any tiny air bubbles that may become trapped under the decal. Only several drops will be required.

(6) Ensure that the surface of the model is secure, then holding the backing sheet, slide the decal into its correct position using the soft sable. Further drops of Superset may be needed to 'float' the decal into its correct position.

(7) Apply Supersol over the positioned decal. Soon it will curl and wrinkle — but don't touch it! The liquid will soften the decal so that it conforms exactly with the surface beneath.

(8) As the decal slowly dries it will flatten and shrink adhering firmly to any surface — even this corrugated Form Trimotor wing.

(9) When dry examine the decal for air bubbles. If present, prick with a sharp pin and reapply Supersol. Repeat the process as necessary.

(10) When decals have set for 24 hours, wash model gently with warm water then apply extra varnish for overall smooth finish.

Chapter 12

THE FINE ART OF AIRBRUSHING

Webster's 3rd new International Dictionary defines the airbrush as: 'An often pencil shaped atomiser for applying, by compressed air, a fine spray of paint, protective coating, or liquid colour, as in shading, drawing, retouching photographs etc.'

The rather stylised description covers a multitude of sins that require a journey back to the turn of the century to uncover fully.

In 1893 Mr. C.L. BURDICK invented the first paint spraying device which relied on the movement of a needle valve to control fluid flow. This was to lead to the forming of the Aerograph company. Aerograph is nowadays synonymous with spray painting just as Biro is to ball-point pens and Hoover is to vacuum cleaners.

About the same time as this major breakthrough Dr. Alan DeVilbiss, an American medical practitioner, devised the first nose and throat atomiser using a rubber bulb and a glass bottle.

Both Aerograph and DeVilbiss moved in their own different directions until 1909 when DeVilbiss produced the world's first spray gun. Spray painting had arrived!

During the First World War both companies expanded but the next major breakthrough occurred in 1923 when the American Dupont company introduced quick-drying lacquer to the motor industry. This removed a major bottleneck in production plants where previously cars were left for many hours to dry between coats.

During the years much friendly technical interchange had taken place between Aerograph and DeVilbiss and it was not really surprising therefore in 1931 to see the amalgamation of the two companies although it was not until 1966 that the UK company finally adopted the DeVilbiss name. To this day the handbuilt Aerograph airbrushes such as Super 63 series are regarded by many as the standard by which airbrushes are judged. That is not to say of course that they have had it all their own way. Many other companies with worldwide reputations now exist in the spraying field. Neither are these reputations restricted to painting. Although much of the development time and money goes to improving paint applications many other less obvious areas are also covered (!) by these companies. French polish on furniture, glaze on

Efbe B2 airbrush with side bowl. Lid to latter is not always standard with other brushes, a shame, as this avoids accidental spillage.

china, gloss on tea buns and meat pies, speckles on Easter eggs, reflective surfaces on cinema screens, all result from advances in spraying technology. Not only liquids but powders, plastics, and fibre glass are now regularly applied by spray in the world's industries.

Whether it is moisture sprayed into tobacco, vitamins into cereals, salt onto peanuts or adhesive onto labels, modern spray equipment can supply the answer. Large computerised spray plants can cover many coloured application to massed produced consumer goods at a speed and accuracy unmatched by hand spraying.

Despite all this, the basic principle of the Aerograph is still in use by many manufacturers to provide the commercial artist with the extra degree of

One of the latest needleless guns, the Model 350 from Badger with 2 oz and 4 oz jars, aerosol can valve/cap, hose and side bowl.

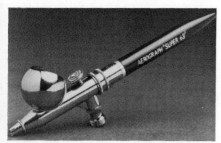

One of the most well known airbrushes, the Aerograph/Devillbiss "Super 63" a well proven design with a long pedigree.

finesse that his profession demands.

With all the backing of such a vast industry it is not surprising that the discerning modeller has become a spray addict. Unfortunately modellers are renowned to be both ultra conservative and, to an extent, penny pinching, and for some years only the specialists painted with air. The advent of a rapidly growing plastic kit industry, however, brought a new dimension to this requirement and many of us sought to paint our newly acquired creation with soft 'feathered' edges to the camouflage. Some of us invested a fortune in commercial art-style airbrushes and persevered until we were proficient. Then came the affluent era and suddenly an airbrush became a status symbol and soon no self respecting modeller would be seen without one.

With this new-found gadget wonders could be performed — or could they? Still the serious modeller produced the results, but to Mr. Average it was a tale of disillusion. Airbrushes were returned (and to that matter still are!) to suppliers and complaints that they did not work. Many had been damaged through mis-

handling but many more were found to be faultless — the fault lying in the inability of the user to obtain the best from the unit. The secret, it appeared, was that few had taken the trouble to practise and practise and practise until a satisfactory level of expertise was attained *before* painting their favourite model.

Well we can overcome this problem by trying to understand how the airbrush works, then applying the practice principles through a series of easy-to-do exercises.

Basically there are three approaches to airbrush design, all of which are perfectly valid. Each approach has its advantages and its snags and as we progress you will be able to ascertain which gun is best suited to your job. The selection of the airbrush is of paramount importance in that it must match as nearly as possible the job in hand. It is of no use for instance buying the DeVilbiss Sprite to paint your 6ft R/C Biplane. Similarly the Binks-Bullows 920 is not suitable for detailing a 1/72nd scale Spitfire.

The three styles of design are:

(1) Twin action needle
(2) Single Action needle
(3) Needle-less

By far the most sophisticated airbrushes are the twin action needle type (and usually the most expensive). In general a far greater degree of finesse can be obtained with this type of instrument and it is this type that is widely used in graphic art studios. Small detail spraying, such as is encountered in plastic

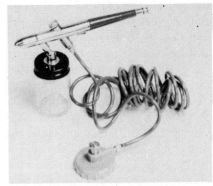

One of the latest Badgers, a 200 EX with needle adjustment screws positioned outside of shank.

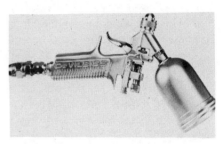

Devillbiss MP Spray gun, ideal for larger models of aircraft and boats.

Compressors come in assorted sizes from various sources. Make quite sure that one you choose is capable of keeping up with your airbrush or spraygun.

kits, often demands this degree of control and if finance allows, this is the area you should investigate. Airbrushes such as the DeVilbiss Sprite and Sprite Major Badger 100 and 150 series fall into this category but it should be noted that several well-established manufacturers are not represented in modelling circles. Airbrushes like the Paasche from the USA, Efbe from Germany and Olympos, Rich & Iwata from Japan may be found in commercial art stockists at realistic prices, so be prepared to shop around. It is also not surprising to see imports from Taiwan and Korea taking a slice of this market at some-

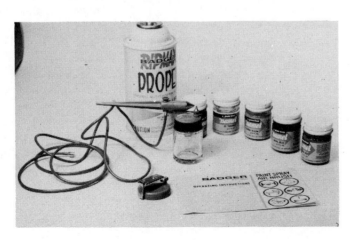

Right, Badger 250 Spray gun, not technically an airbrush as there is no needle. Behind is typical Aerosol propellant can, not as economical as a compressor. Pactra enamels in background.

what more budget prices. Twin action airbrushes can control both airflow and paint flow by different movements of the same control button. Obviously this type of airbrush requires considerably more practice to become proficient.

Single acting needle brushes fill a most useful area of spray painting and a great deal of the larger sprayguns are built to this pattern. These units are not usually quite so complex as the twin action airbrushes, and are usually a little cheaper and easier to use. The prime difference lies in the fact that paint flow may be adjusted by moving a *separate* control to that used in painting. It is customary to adjust this paint control before, rather than during, a spray operation. The essence of the twin action brush being that you can adjust paint flow during spraying with the *same* control knob that you are using to spray as just stated.

Airbrushes such as the Badger 200 and larger guns such as the Aerograph MP and the Binks-Bullows L900 and 920 series make use of this single action feature. Although to be fair, the larger sprayguns still retain the control of paint flow *while spraying* — a feature absent from the Model 200. Needle-less guns, as their name suggests, have no needle but draw paint from the reservoir by suction obtained by blowing air across the top of an open jet. Early scent sprays used this technique. The Celspray unit of some years back, operated by a handheld bulb, started the whole model spraying business off.

It is fair to say that this type of unit, while cheaper to make, does not have the degree of control or the finesse of output of the other two styles. The exception to this being units like the Binks-Bullow Wren and the Badger 350 where this state of the art has been brought to the ultimate.

Many cheap guns such as the Brown Hobby gun, Badger 250 and Humbrol offer a simple and quick answer to the modeller requiring a greater area of cover.

Greater areas of cover still, such as base colours on large flying models, would benefit from the commercial single action needle guns mentioned

earlier.

It must be apparent by now that the spray painting scene is a horses-for-courses situation and it is not uncommon to find the more serious modeller possessing two or more spray units to cover the wide range of his requirements.

Whatever your requirements it must be remembered that any spraygun, and particularly the finer airbrushes, are delicate instruments produced to a very exacting standard and do not take kindly to misuse. Do not chuck them in your toolbox at the end of a spraying session, but *carefully* clean them following the manufacturers instructions and put them away in their cases.

By now you will be completely confused about the choice of airbrush, but you have bought one anyhow — what next?

Any airbrush or spraygun is only as good as its air supply. To achieve any form of consistent result requires a consistent source of pressure. The advent of the aerosol can has enabled many modellers, whose use of an airbrush is somewhat intermittent, to acquire a cheap form of pressure. However, for all serious use, the aerosol is not really suited. Primarily because in the long term it becomes an expensive way of satisfying the requirement, particularly if you realise that, for anything other than intermittent use, the pressure change occurring in the can during use is a source of embarrassment. Pressure regulators added to the can or immersion of the can in warm water (careful!) are temporary ways to combat the problem, but do not really get to the source of the matter.

Spare wheels (inner tubes) from a car also suffer from constantly falling pressure during use, although as a stopgap this technique is sometimes useful. It is, after all, a cheap source and both Badger and Humbrol produce adaptors to fit a car tyre valve.

By far the best approach to this problem is the compressor, although the hire of an air cylinder is also worth investigating. Many artists' studios use compressed air or carbon dioxide cylinders. The rental (on a returnable

deposit system) is quite low although the initial deposit is high. Usage on a pence per cu ft basis is quite acceptable and as, each cylinder has its own pressure regulator, an exact and *constant* pressure may be achieved.

Commercial compressors tend to be very expensive, the recognised manufacturers charging many hundreds of pounds. Many modellers have successfully manufactured their own units from such ex-WD equipment as truck tyre pumps driven by washing machine motors. Pressure vessels, regulators, safety valves etc. can often be obtained from truck braking systems from the same ex-WD source. Ex-refrigerator compressors can usually be obtained quite cheaply from refrigeration repair dealers and pressure vessels can be made from fire extinguishers, Calor gas bottles, etc. Fixtures and fittings may be obtained from your nearest pneumatics dealer — check your *Yellow Pages*! Whatever you choose to do be careful — compressed air can be very dangerous.

Several useful commercial compressors (suitable only for small airbrushes) are available on the model market and while offering good value for money, lack the finesse needed to provide the widest use. Low flow rates make them eminently suited to the airbrush but unable to cope with the larger guns. Most notable of these is the well-established Badger. These units may be regulated to a given pressure by the retro fitting of a pressure regulator and may have an oil/moisture trap fitted. Even so the resulting air supply pulsates rather than being steady. However once conversant with its use, no trouble should be experienced with this pulsing air supply. Indeed some of the finest airbrushing seen applied to models has been accomplished with these units. The American Brown Corporation produce two compressors, one similar to the Badger and one much smaller, simpler and of course cheaper. Neither of the Brown units are really fully adjustable, although for a great amount of users they would be adequate as would that from Badger mentioned previously.

The serious student of airbrush techniques should note these comments for to obtain the practice necessary to make perfect, a *great quantity* of air will be consumed and the cost of all this practice needs to be measured in the soundest terms.

What next then? The airbrush and air supply to hand, what about all this practice? Obtain an artist's sketch pad and try these simple exercises.

(1) Rule the page with horizontal pencil lines full page width and about ½″ (38.1mm) apart. Using an arm movement (not wrist), learn to spray across the page from both left and right hand margins such that each pencil line is covered with a line of watercolour or ink, approx 1″ (25.4mm) wide. The object is to learn to control the paint flow, to keep the gun moving parallel to the paper and not in an arc and to be able to reproduce a given width of spray along a given line. When satisfied with the result, repeat the exercise with a spray of say about ⅜″ (19.5mm) width and finally with a spray of about ¹⁄₁₆″ (2mm) width.

When you can fill a sheet of paper with parallel lines of paint, from the left or the right and all lines are of the same width and paint density then you are beginning to achieve success.

(2) Try a clean sheet of rule paper and make each pass of the airbrush wide, medium, fine, wide, medium, etc. until the page is full. Are all of the lines straight? Do they follow the pencil line? Is each thick line the same width? and each medium line? and each fine line? They are? Good, then you are beginning to acquire the necessary control. Try now to render tones.

(3) Take your clean sheet of paper and mask off all around the edge with 1″ (25.4mm) masking tape. Using alternate left and right strokes, lightly spray the entire exposed area with a wash of pale paint. Remove the mask and you should have an even block of pale colour with no streaks or blotches. You haven't? Try again until you can achieve an even cover. You can then go on to trying a graded wash from solid colour at the bottom of the masked off area, fading through to pure white at the top.

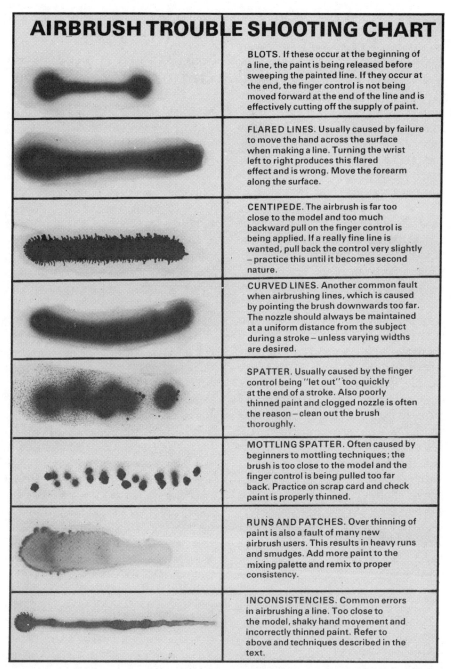

AIRBRUSH TROUBLE SHOOTING CHART

BLOTS. If these occur at the beginning of a line, the paint is being released before sweeping the painted line. If they occur at the end, the finger control is not being moved forward at the end of the line and is effectively cutting off the supply of paint.

FLARED LINES. Usually caused by failure to move the hand across the surface when making a line. Turning the wrist left to right produces this flared effect and is wrong. Move the forearm along the surface.

CENTIPEDE. The airbrush is far too close to the model and too much backward pull on the finger control is being applied. If a really fine line is wanted, pull back the control very slightly – practice this until it becomes second nature.

CURVED LINES. Another common fault when airbrushing lines, which is caused by pointing the brush downwards too far. The nozzle should always be maintained at a uniform distance from the subject during a stroke – unless varying widths are desired.

SPATTER. Usually caused by the finger control being "let out" too quickly at the end of a stroke. Also poorly thinned paint and clogged nozzle is often the reason – clean out the brush thoroughly.

MOTTLING SPATTER. Often caused by beginners to mottling techniques; the brush is too close to the model and the finger control is being pulled too far back. Practice on scrap card and check paint is properly thinned.

RUNS AND PATCHES. Over thinning of paint is also a fault of many new airbrush users. This results in heavy runs and smudges. Add more paint to the mixing palette and remix to proper consistency.

INCONSISTENCIES. Common errors in airbrushing a line. Too close to the model, shaky hand movement and incorrectly thinned paint. Refer to above and techniques described in the text.

Each of these exercises is an essential step in trying to become fully conversant with the use of your own airbrush. Do not give up for only with this practice will you be able to progress to those fabulous finishes seen on the experts' models.

One of the basic techniques of airbrushing is the rendering of solid 3-dimensional objects on a flat surface. Again practice exercises are essential. Try to mask off a rectangle either horizontal or vertical and shade it to look like a cylinder, remove the mask and take a look — do it again if not satisfied.

Other shapes such as a cube or sphere may be attempted in a similar manner. The sphere is largely a matter of gun control on a simple mask while the cube requires three separate masks, one for each face. Note how the faces of the cube all have a different shade and how the shade varies across the face of the cube.

With all this practice a great degree of control will emerge as will the knowledge that a good reliable air source is money well spent.

Masking off is an integral part of the airbrushing scene and no article would be complete without reference to *Friskets*.

Friskets, to the modeller, are simple transparent masks that can be easily separated with a sharp knife to enable part of the mask to be removed. Several proprietary self-adhesive films are available from artists' suppliers (although rarely seen in model shops), Friskfilm and Magic Marker film being two which come readily to mind. From modelling suppliers look for film from Badger and Revell. Transpaseal is a good substitute however and is cheaper, although it is somewhat more sticky and may adhere too strongly with the subsequent removal of the base coat of paint. Transpaseal is available from most big stationers where it is sold for covering books etc. for protection. The beauty of Frisket films is that parts of the required pattern may be cut out with a sharp knife and sprayed through as a stencil. When dry the cut-out pieces may be returned to the hole and adjacent pieces removed to add a different colour or shade. Quite complex patterns and designs can be obtained by the 'cut out and replace' technique. Roundels, squadron crests, serial numbers and a myriad of other details can be applied in this manner.

Conventional masking tape may be used for the more coarse masking on larger types of models backed up by the usual application of newspaper. Often masking tape may be obtained $\frac{1}{16}$" (2mm) or $\frac{1}{8}$" (4mm) which will negotiate compound curves with ease, allowing the basic line to be produced, backed up again with newspaper. Paint is known to 'creep' under masking tape unless care is applied when pressing down the tape thoroughly. There are, of course, times when one cannot press too hard (for instance tissue-covered free-flight scale models). Another handy dodge to use here is to spray the first coat over the edge of the mask with the same colour as that *below* the mask. Therefore any creep will be the same as the existing colour and will not show. This action effectively seals the edge of the tape and subsequent applications of differing colour can be achieved in safety. When removing the mask always pull back

gently along the mask rather than pull at right angles to the painted surface.

COMPATIBILITY OF MATERIALS

Materials used in scale model finishing vary tremendously but whatever type is used, the correct consistency is essential to satisfactory spraying. Cellulose (colour dope) is still the most widely used finishing material for flying models although enamels are used and polyurethanes and epoxy paints are finding greater acceptance. Acrylic lacquers, while having much to commend them, not the least being the almost limitless range of colours, do not seem to have caught on. Plastic kits are almost inevitably painted with enamels or their immediate derivatives. Enamels and cellulose do not mix. Neither do their thinning agents. Probably the most widely used (but by no means the only) finish for plastic are the Humbrol and Revell ranges, although newer speciality paints like Extra Colour and Precision Paints are gaining in popularity. These and other enamels may, if desired, be applied *over* a cellulose finish but not the other way round.

Cellulose and plastic (polystyrene to be precise) do not go together. Cellulose thinner dissolves plastic kits. Despite this, deft use of the airbrush with its fine mist spray will enable cellulose to be applied to the plastic kit provided only light coats are used. The rapid evaporation of the cellulose thinners allow the paint to dry before the thinners attack the surface of the plastic, although a primer is advisable where cross kitting or modifications produce mixed standards of surface finish.

In actual fact a very slight attack

Above, R/C Spitfire undergoing filling and sanding prior to priming and airbrushing. Careful preparation is vital for spray painting of any kind.

always does take place but this is rarely visible to the naked eye and in fact serves to 'key' the colour to the plastic.

Whether spraying cellulose or enamel you should consider the health hazard and not spray near open flame. *Always* wear a face mask. If you do not believe me, take a mask element apart after a couple of hours of spraying and see for yourself the colour inside it. That would have all gone into your lungs!! More exotic finishes like epoxy and polyurethanes are a greater hazard and should be treated even more carefully. Many flying models are finished in these products these days, either as a colourant or purely as a clear protective lacquer to stop the ingress of raw fuel and exhaust waste — K & B Super Poxy and Ripmax Tufcote being of particular interest. Super Poxy is attractive to the scale modeller as it is available in matt

Right, method of sanding balsa wood during preparation of flying scale model for painting. All grain needs to be filled and a really smooth appearance achieved.

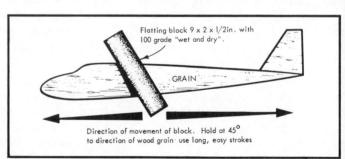

Flatting block 9 x 2 x 1/2in. with 100 grade "wet and dry".

GRAIN

Direction of movement of block. Hold at 45° to direction of wood grain use long, easy strokes

finish clear, which provides a most authentic dull appearance on, for instance, WW2 models. Regrettably it has been found that the matt epoxy is not so fuel-proof as the gloss and many modellers now prefer to gloss finish with an extra coat or two and flat down with steel wool or fine wet and dry paper.

Techniques on scale models vary enormously but it is fair to say that these shown in the accompanying photographs are fairly typical, both in base colour application and in detail.

To illustrate the point, consider the R/C Spitfire and Me109 models that were entirely tissue covered and clear doped, and carefully prepared.

PREPARATION

Before you even start to consider the spraying or brush painting of any model the surfaces must be prepared. We have already touched upon this when discussing plastic kits, but for flying powered models obviously quite different approaches are needed. Covering of flying scale models is usually either with tissue, silk or nylon depending on your personal preferences or type of model you are building. Usually silk or nylon finished models are not difficult to prepare as several coats of dope, ideally

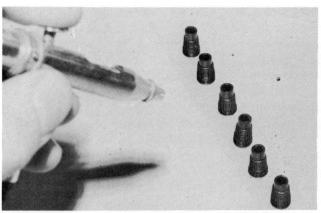

When spraying small items i.e. separate engine cylinders for a Peanut scale model as shown here, double sided tape can be used. The pieces to be sprayed are attached firmly to the tape which in turn is secured to stiff card or similar. Spraying can now commence, usually the area held by the tape will be the cementing area, so this trick serves as a double purpose in that it also saves scraping away excess paint prior to gluing.

sanding between carefully with fine wet and dry paper, is usually sufficient to fill the weave of the material — always assuming of course that the wooden airframe has been doped and smoothed down first.

With tissue there is the possibility that doping will lift some of the fibres and a 'hairy' appearance will result. This can be cured, by leaving the model to dry before wiping — not rubbing — the surface with dry 1200 grade silica carbide paper (wet and dry). Removal of the fibres completed, a final application of clear dope will suffice and colouring can commence with whatever type of finish you choose.

The painting of sheet balsa wood components such as fuselages and tailplanes needs careful preparation, per-

haps more so that any other form of surface, as obviously splits, grain, pinholes, joints etc. must be filled after construction and instant tube Polyfilla is ideal for larger irregularities and Fine Surface Polyfilla for less obvious ones. Modern proprietary fillers like M.D. Superfiller also produce superb results. These fillers are perfectly compatible with balsa (plastics too) and have the advantage of quick drying and easy sanding properties. General rubbing down of balsa is best achieved with dry wet and dry paper mounted on a sanding block with double-sided tape.

Always follow the directions on the grain when smoothing and carefully finish curves, fillets, etc. with handheld paper, remembering to rub in long easy strokes. After the balsa has been smoothed as much as possible, apply tissue and at least two coats of cellulose clear dope, carefully sanding between each application. After this has dried colour decoration can take place.

An even finer finish on sheet areas can be obtained by spraying a coat of grey primer, such as manufactured for the automotive industry, and after this has dried spray a coat of colour preferably in a different shade to that of the primer. When this has dried, sand the model again using 280 grade wet and dry paper wetted and continued until removal of the colour coat has been achieved. If any of the colour is still evident it is obvious that this indicates a flaw or crack which needs filling with Stopper and sanding smooth again. It should be applied by fingers (wear a rubber glove) or flexible spatula and carefully worked into the crack.

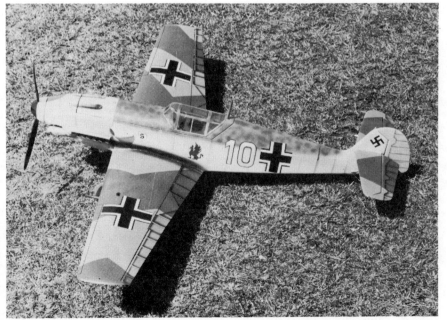

Above, the author's Me109e completely airbrushed.

The idea of the colour coat is to reveal any imperfection after sanding and has a similar function to the primer used for plastic models to indicate proper filling. Twenty-four hours must now elapse before the model is finally dusted, wiped with an anti-static duster and painted. In the case of our Spitfire it was decided that the Squadron codes were to be in the same colour as the underside and accordingly the fuselage sides were also sprayed. The gun used for this base coat (and also the primer) was the DeVilbiss MP. Although the Binks-Bullows L900 was also used for the Me109 with equally satisfactory results.

When completely dry, the underside was checked for streaks or runs (and rectified where necessary). Masking tape was used to separate the lower colour using newspaper for large areas. No tape was used at L.E. or T.E. of wings and tailplane preferring instead to use the gun at right angles to the required surface allowing a 'natural' edge to form. Squadron letters were cut from masking tape and applied firmly. The upper surface (Ocean Grey) was applied using the same gun. The Dark Green camouflage was added (without waiting for the grey to dry) using a Badger 200. This was gilding the lily as the MP gun was perfectly adequate for this type of feather-edge work, but the Badger

already had green in it and it was easier to swap guns than to clean out and change colour. The upper surfaces were allowed to dry thoroughly and the masking removed (except for canopy). Canopy masking stays on until last allowing camouflage and any other detail (oil stains etc.) to extend across the framework. Detail masking was added for such areas as yellow L.E. to wings and Sky type 'S' band around rear fuselage. Back-up was again newspaper. Coloured cellulose was used throughout for all colouring. When this detail was dry the masking was removed

Above, correctly applied mottle to this two-seat Me262 has proven the advantage of owning an airbrush, authentic rendering of this camouflage is almost impossible to achieve by any other means. Below, Ray Habgood's superb "Chevy" van entirely airbrushed with Badger Equipment. Careful masking, plenty of skill, and constant practise is required for this sort of effect.

and still smaller detail added. Machine gun patches were masked and using a Sprite or similar, red dope applied. When dry, the machine gun holes were bored into the L.E.using a round needle file. Caution in removing this file leaves slivers of balsa standing proud of the edge of the hole. Using very Dark Grey paint a quick squirt of the Sprite into the hole effectively sealed these slivers in place producing a smoke-blackened tattered edge to the hole. Exhausts were airbrushed with a mixture of Black and Copper and exhaust stains added from Dark Grey. Roundels were not, in fact, airbrushed on this model (a sad admission really) but applied with Humbrol matt enamel (suitably darkened). Draughtsman's compasses with an ink pen were used to mark the inner and outer edges of the colours which were filled in with a brush.

Not so on the Me109 however, the markings were drawn onto proprietary masking film and applied to the airframe. Carefully cutting away the white areas, these were sprayed with cellulose from the airbrush.

While these were drying similar Friskets were made for the shield and the dragon emblems. Again these were airbrushed in with colour dope from the Sprite. The removed parts of Frisket were replaced, effectively covering the white areas, and the black areas removed, airbrushing through the resulting mask. Finally the entire Frisket was removed and presto — airbrushed markings. Much more satisfying (and more accurate in most cases) than using a waterslide transfer.

Both Spitfire and Messerschmitt (full-size that is) had fabric-covered elevators and rudders. To achieve this in model form is not difficult but with simple models like these a solid balsa structure is utilised. It therefore fell to the paint job to duplicate the appearance of fabric covering. Accordingly all the rib positions were covered (chordwise obviously) with $\frac{1}{16}$" (2mm) masking tape. The outline of the metal leading edge was cut from 1" (25.4mm) masking tape and applied to the surface in question. Using a twin action airbrush a light dusting of colour was applied to the edge of the mask creating the 'shadow' effect so noticeable in the full size. Gentle application is required for it is easy to produce an over-done image. Choice of colour is a prime point in producing a subtle effect. Avoid black wherever possible. A light or mid-grey is probably best depending on the base colour. On the underside of, say, an Me109 or similar, a shade or two darker than the underside colour would be quite suitable. Remember it is subtlety that we are seeking — do not attack it with sledgehammer blows!!

Panel lines on the Spitfire were achieved by using narrow black tape. This is made for the preparation of printed circuit artwork and come in a vast range of sizes and colours. Look for it in commercial art suppliers. The Me109 panels were sprayed by masking the panel line with 1" (25.4mm) tape and gently airbrushing over the edge of tape. Try to overspray onto the model by the barest amount ($\frac{1}{16}$" (2mm) is ample).

Finally, just the slightest trace of grey was airbrushed around air intakes, radiators etc. The Me109 gun troughs were similarly treated.

The underside of the Spitfire's wings had the cartridge ejector chutes added with the aid of a Frisket. Carbon deposits were blown in freehand in Dark Grey and were rather over-done. As mentioned earlier, a gentle, subtle effect, is more in keeping.

The entire finished airframe was sprayed with Tufcote using again the larger gun. Scrupulous cleanliness is essential when producing this type of finish and it is a good habit to get into. Clean each gun as you use it and put it away. Do not leave them lying around to be damaged. This is particularly important when using two part resins such as Tufcote etc.

Summarising therefore:

(1) Choose the gun or airbrush with care to ensure that you obtain the correct type for the job in hand. Check out adaptability features such as interchangeable jets for different degrees of paint coverage.

(2) Use the best possible back-up facility. Money spent on compressors with oil and moisture filters and regulated outputs is an investment that will be repaid many times over.

(3) Practice, practice, practice. Where possible visit local colleges and schools of art. Learn how to control the airbrush or gun until precision and accuracy become second nature.

(4) Choose paint types to suit your model and try to stick to one type throughout. Avoid mixing paint types wherever possible.

(5) BE AWARE OF SAFETY REQUIREMENTS. Wear a mask — *always* — and avoid spraying adjacent to naked flame.

(6) Above all, treat the airbrush and spraygun with respect. They are delicate instruments which with proper care will last you a lifetime and never wear out. Clean them *immediately* after use following the manufacturers instructions. Put them away after use.

SOURCES OF EQUIPMENT

Airbrushes: Twin action needle type

Badger 100 Series
Badger 150
DeVilbiss Sprite and Sprite Major
Kager
Powermax
Obtainable through most model shops.

DeVilbiss Super 63 Series
Paasche Series
Efbe Series
Iwata
Olympos
Rich

Royal Sovereign
Usually available through commercial art dealers.

Airbrushes: Single action
needle type
Badger 200
Available from model shops.

Airbrushes: Needle-less type

Humbrol
Badger 350
Badger 250
Brown hobby gun
Available from model shops

Binks-Bullows Wren
Obtainable from industrial spray equipment stockists.

Note the Humbrol gun has no connection to fit a compressor. It may only be used with Aerosols or motor tyres.
The Badger 350 may be used on quite fine work more usually associated with needle airbrushes.
The Binks-Bullow Wren has 3 interchangeable jets covering a wide range of uses but cannot be used with the finesse of small airbrushes.

Sprayguns: Larger types for flying models etc.

DeVilbiss MP
DeVilbiss MPS
Binks-Bullows L900
Binks-Bullows 920
Available from industrial paint spraying stockists.

Aerosols:

Humbrol
Frisk
Morris & Ingram
Magic Marker
Roughly comparable price per oz. Available from model shops and other sources (e.g. Halfords etc.), (prices vary).

Compressors:

Badger
Brown
Royal Sovereign etc.
Available from model shops or graphic art suppliers.

DIY units — most parts can be obtained (together with free advice) from pneumatic suppliers. Check with *Yellow Pages*. Ask for well-known brandnames such as Schrader and Wade etc.

Accessories:

Transpaseal	Stationers
Frisk Film	Art Suppliers
Magic Marker Film	
Revell & Badger film	Model shops
Masking tape	Art Suppliers

Note Extra thin masking tape together with 'special' American paints such as Metalflake can also be obtained from Denis Ferney, (for Metalflake address see page 49). Also many fancy finishing extras including Japanese airbrushes and decorative and refractive tapes may be obtained from this specialist source.

Chapter 13

ONE MAN'S APPROACH TO AIRBRUSHING

BEFORE YOU START

(1) Select the airbrush — I started work with the Badger 250 model, but found it insufficiently sensitive or versatile so thereafter used a Badger 200. So start with the best you can afford, remembering that both wide spray and fine line capability will eventually be required and may even lead to the need for two or more guns.

(2) The compressor is a very expensive item, but should be judged carefully against the cost of aerosol cans. My first airbrushed 1/32nd model, a Revell Phantom, used four large cans; after that, I then bought a compressor! I can strongly recommend it as it gives a steady pressure for as long as you want for many years to come. It also overcomes the urge to rush, brought about by the thought of those £5 notes blowing out of the window!

(3) You may have seen commercial airbrush demonstrations at exhibitions, where tiny areas are sprayed with the thinnest of paint. In which case you will disbelieve me when I claim that airbrushing is messy, smelly and, (if you have a compressor) noisy, unless you use the more expensive silent versions. The overspray does get everywhere, and it colours kitchen extract fans quite delightfully. Make sure you have a quiet, well-ventilated area where you can practice the art, without getting evicted from the household. However, you will find that as your con-

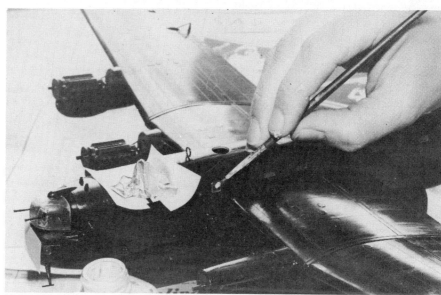

Masking of clear area is achieved either by commercial liquid masking or PVA adhesive. For large openings, damp tissue paper can be squeezed into place.

fidence and expertise grows, the mess gets less, but beginners: *beware*.

(4) To avoid frustration, first realise that most models will take much longer to finish using an airbrush. Masking, setting-up and cleaning all takes considerable time — longer than the actual painting in fact. You will also need to exercise quite a lot of care in pre-planning the final assembly and colouring sequence of the model.

(5) You must take things slowly and calmly; you must keep everything absolutely clean; you must be prepared to stop, clean-up and start afresh if things go wrong; you must practice. Use an old model or a kit bought for the purpose and practice masking, spraying different patterns and colour divisions.

If you pick up an airbrush for the first time to spray your 'perfect' model, I guarantee that you will regret it, even if you avoid a nervous breakdown.

ASSEMBLY OF THE MODEL

In spite of the above, I assume you have decided to proceed, so let's take a more positive view of the matter.

(1) Generally, all the major components of your model can be assembled as normal. But since airbrushing gives a very thin paint film, any faults will be glaringly apparent, so take extra care. Undercoats should be applied to scratch-built areas to match the base plastic colour, finishing it off with a piece of very worn, fine wet and dry

paper. This means you can achieve a consistent final colour to the model with less spraying.

(2) The 'add-on' parts of the model should be sprayed separately and assembled afterwards. These include underwing stores, dive brakes, 'drooped' flaps, open cockpit canopies and u/c doors. If you don't adopt this course you will run into extensive masking difficulties and may find that you cannot easily get the paint to cover all surfaces.

(3) Some interior surfaces are impossible to airbrush once the model is complete, yet cannot be fitted after painting, i.e. jet intakes and wheel wells. You will have to spray or brush paint them at an early stage, filling the cavity with damp tissue paper, and sealing round the edge with Maskol or similar. It is easier in many cases to omit the undercarriage entirely until spraying is complete, provided you can arrange for simple and secure fixing at the appropriate time.

(4) Make sure at an early stage, that any parts to be fitted after airbrushing can be attached cleanly and accurately. Many kits provide for undercarriage doors to be stuck directly to the aircraft skin, which is unrealistic and unsatisfactory. Consider 'dummy' hinges and the means you will use to effect a bond. Five minute epoxy or cyanoacrylates are best in my experience, they bond onto paint and don't attack the surfaces.

MASKING THE MODEL

(1) The materials used for masking are as follows:

(a) Masking tape available at stationers and hardware shops.
(b) Lining tape, which is usually very narrow ($\frac{1}{16}$" or ⅛" and is available from draughtsman's supplies.
(c) Masking film, which is clear sheet or tape and can be obtained from large modelling suppliers.
(d) Masking fluid (i.e. Maskol) or PVA adhesive which is a liquid rubbery substance, from most model shops.
(e) Sellotape.
(f) Paper, either normal weight or tissue.
(g) Thin card.

(2) Unless considerable care is exercised and the tape pre-used, masking tape and Sellotape are too strong and will tend to pull the paint underneath them away. They can be used satisfactorily on bare plastic of course.

(3) The masking film, being 'low tack', is much better but care is still necessary when removing it. The slightest grease on the model, left prior to spraying, will accentuate the tendency of the paint to lift off. Similar comments apply to the lining tape, which is very useful to mask off over-complex shapes. Use it to set the edge of the line, then complete the

job with film or fluid.

(4) When using tape or film, (except lining tape), to get a straight edge colour line, always cut a new edge onto the medium with a sharp blade and steel rule.

(5) Masking fluid is the most generally useful medium of them all. Obviously your 'edge' will only be as accurate as you can brush the fluid on. If you use it to cover, say, the entire undersurface of a model, be careful how you pull it off. It comes off in one piece and can easily take a few aerials, etc. off with it. It also sheds flakes of paint as it contracts — if these are still soft they can attach themselves fairly tenaciously to just where you don't want them. One fault of the fluid is that it tends to pull out from under the paint, round the edges of the area. This is worst with gloss paint and leaves you with a ragged edge of loose paint, which has to be carefully removed with a sharpened matchstick, or similar, dipped in a little thinners. It can also cause slight yellowing of white paint. PVA does none of these.

(6) A 'soft' colour division can be sprayed freehand, using a handheld card mask for safety, if you have the skill and a suitable 'fine line' capability to your particular airbrush. If not you will need to arrange your mask a little way distant from the surface to be painted to allow some overspray. On fuselage, the card mask can be fastened with masking

Above, after the upper colours, next the black for this 1/48th Lancaster. Mask upper areas using tape and a liquid medium as shown left. The masking is finally removed (right) to reveal the complete scheme. Final varnish will darken the lightened colours (thanks to thinning) and restore them to their correct hues.

MASKING HINTS

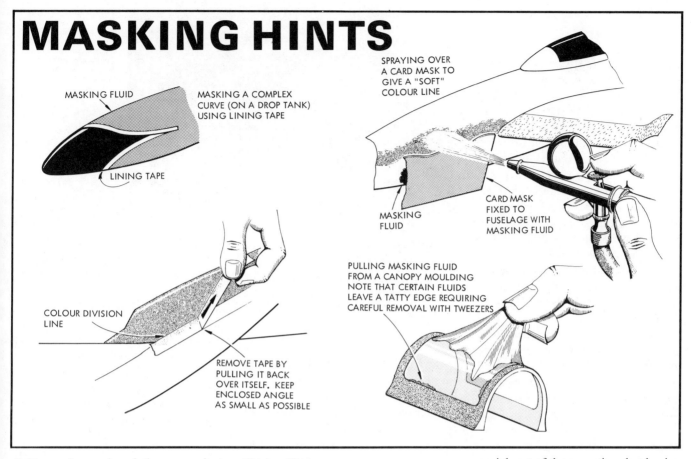

MASKING FLUID

MASKING A COMPLEX CURVE (ON A DROP TANK) USING LINING TAPE

LINING TAPE

SPRAYING OVER A CARD MASK TO GIVE A "SOFT" COLOUR LINE

MASKING FLUID

CARD MASK FIXED TO FUSELAGE WITH MASKING FLUID

COLOUR DIVISION LINE

REMOVE TAPE BY PULLING IT BACK OVER ITSELF. KEEP ENCLOSED ANGLE AS SMALL AS POSSIBLE

PULLING MASKING FLUID FROM A CANOPY MOULDING NOTE THAT CERTAIN FLUIDS LEAVE A TATTY EDGE REQUIRING CAREFUL REMOVAL WITH TWEEZERS

fluid on the angle of the curve just below the desired colour line.

(7) You need not waste tape or fluid to mask large areas, just use them to get the edge accurate, then fix a large piece of paper in place over the rest using masking fluid. (The fluid makes a very useful 'glue' for holding things temporarily, since it can be easily removed without marking the surfaces concerned.)

(8) Some models benefit from the use of special metallic finishes, (i.e. Rub n' Buff or Liqua-Plate). You cannot use any masking medium on these, except masking fluid if handled carefully. Remember that if you apply one of these finishes adjacent to paint, you will not be able to buff it without spoiling the other colour. I use these finishes in two ways; either small areas of Rub n' Buff (mixed with another colour as necessary), applied before airbrushing the model, masked off with fluid, *or* paint and mask the non-metallic areas of a 'natural metal' aircraft and spray Liqua-Plate overall. These comments do *not* apply to the use of SnJ (see

Chapter 3).

(9) A final word on masking, do take your time and do a comprehensive job. It is better than trying to clean off unwanted paint that has found its way onto other areas. Bits of damp tissue or thin paper can easily be attached, using masking fluid, to cover up all the areas you have already painted.

SPRAYING THE MODEL

You are now ready to commence the

crucial part of the operation, but having first practised as advised.

(1) When mixing your paint, the final consistency should be such that a drop, placed on a vertical glass surface (i.e. inside the paint jar), runs down freely but leaves a strong 'tail' of colour.

(2) Keep the paint control of your brush turned well down and hold the nozzle at least 3″ from the surface. Always keep the brush moving and don't 'start' the spray on the model — make a pass over

Small items such as these engine cylinders can be held by double-sided tape whilst spraying. Usually the surface meeting the tape is the cementing area so the trick serves a double purpose in that it saves scraping away unwanted paint prior to gluing.

the area you are covering to drift on a 'mist' coat. *Never attempt to get a solid coat on in one operation.*

(3) Dust particles will appear like magic on the surface you are spraying, so ensure you clean the model with a soft brush just before you start and that the atmosphere is fairly dust free.

(4) The crunch situation arises when you are halfway through spraying a colour and something goes wrong, i.e. a sudden 'spatter' of lumps of dust etc. appear. There are usually only two courses of action — either complete the job, rubbing down the offending areas when dry and respraying *or* stop at once, wash off the paint, clean up and start again. Trying to wipe off part of the paint or dab off bits of dust is not satisfactory.

(5) A word of warning. If you wash off the offending paint, be careful with the solvents used. Turps attacks plastic quite violently but not immediately. I washed all the paint off a large drop tank and a few hours later it had split almost in half, and not long the cemented join either. Brake fluid is better or one of the proprietary strippers made expressly for plastic kits.

(6) The essence of successful airbrushing is absolute cleanliness of equipment, coupled to the right consistency of paint, with restraint to apply the colour slowly and gradually.

FINISHING THE MODEL

(1) Having carefully removed all masking, don't spoil the effect by getting fingermarks on the model, an old silk handkerchief is my favourite for subsequent handling.

(2) Examine the model for faults, mine seem to come under three headings:

(a) Minute flakes of paint detached with the masking. Clean the area up with very fine, worn wet and dry paper, for a subsequent touch-up, with airbrush set to give minimum spray.

(b) Minor faults or 'runs' of paint at colour division lines, (including the odd tatty edge left by masking fluid). Clean these up with a sharpened matchstick dipped in thinners.

National championships held by the IPMS annually show top examples of airbrush work. This "Aggressors" F-5E in 'Snake' camouflage is no exception. See Aerocolour Tables for paint mix.

(c) Dust, fluff, minor paintwork faults or model faults. The area should be gently rubbed down, using our old friend, the worn wet and dry paper. If necessary, touch-up with the airbrush.

(3) Any slight overspray can usually be removed with the gentle application of metal polish, (i.e. Silvo or Brasso), without damaging the finish.

(4) When you are using your own colour mixes, try and keep some for touching-up work. It is very difficult to repeat mixes for spraying large models, the old eye-dropper method of measuring gets a little tedious.

(5) Some model kits have superb, finely detailed panelling, rivets, inspection cover fastening, etc., usually 'raised'; (a favourite being Hasegawa's 1/32 scale range). If these are rubbed down virtually smooth before spraying, a light application of wet and dry paper afterwards will make the details visible again, but absolutely flush with the paint surface. The effect of this is very subtle and quite pleasing.

(6) Various 'special effect' finishing techniques, like drybrushing, have been well covered elsewhere in this book. However, do try running turps, coloured with a touch of black paint, into control hinge lines, the detail round u/c legs and to highlight nuts and rims on wheels etc. The thin mixture gets carried round the detail by capillary action, so you don't have to be a master hand with the paint brush.

(7) Once the decals are on, you can do subtle weathering, which I prefer to keep to the absolute minimum.

(a) Grated pencil lead (or graphite powder) on the tip of your finger, rubbed over the appropriate area,

Diecast kit of the Comper Swift has been airbrushed over a few coats of Auto Primer cellulose. Trim was masked off with lining tape cut into thin strips, although careful retouching was required later.

PAINT APPLICATION — TROUBLE-SHOOTING

PAINTING PROBLEM	CAUSE AND REMEDY
Brushes shed hairs during painting.	Cheap brushes — throw them away and save up for some better quality ones. If hairs have been applied to the model leave the paint to dry, remove the hair with tweezers — sand smooth with wet and dry paper and repaint.
When painting, lumps and specks of dirt have appeared on the model surface.	Paint has been insufficiently stirred or has reached the end of its life. If a tin is many months old and the paint quite thick it is often best to discard it and restock. Thorough stirring is recommended for all paints prior to application.
Matt paint dries glossy or patchy.	Insufficient stirring again. Remove with car *Brake Fluid* and recoat when surface has been recleaned.
Paint ''skids'' over surface.	Static or mould grease on model — clean with mild detergent and warm water finally wiping over with an *anti-static cloth*.
Second coat drags up first application.	Insufficient drying time allowed between coats. Remove with *Brake Fluid* and recoat. Handle fluid with care.
Removal of masking tape pulls up paint beneath.	Tape too sticky, reduce by rubbing adhesive backing prior to application or pulled away too harshly. Should be removed when paint has dried by doubling back over itself and removing gently and slowly.
First coat is thick, brush drags and uneven surface is obtained.	Paint needs thinning and re-stirring and note that too much thinners will result in general lightening of the colour. Remove with *Brake Fluid* and recoat.
Paint accidentally smudged over clear canopy.	Before it dries remove with a cocktail stick damped with thinners. The latter can cloud the clear part but this is restored by polishing with **Duraglit**.
Paint collects round edges and builds up into a ridge.	When dry, smooth with wet and dry paper recoating with thinned down colour.
Glue dropped on paint surface, accidentally.	Allow to harden, remove with knife, sand smooth and recoat.
Paint brushed over areas to be cemented.	This *must* be scraped off as cement will not work on a painted portion of plastic.

will produce a 'dirty' effect and highlight raised detail, (but only a little).

(b) A *very* fine overspray of thin white or light grey paint will tone down decals or trim colours and produce a faded appearance.

(c) A *very* fine brown/black overspray makes exhaust stains or gun smoke stains.

(d) Allow a little 'dirty' turps to trickle down, where you want to represent fuel or oil leaks.

8) Give the model a final, thin, overpray of appropriate gloss or matt arnish.

And finally, *practice everything first!*

MODEL COLOUR REFERENCES

Colour for Specific Purposes
British Standard 371C: 1964 (UDC 5366) is available from *British Standards House, 2 Park Street, London W1*. The booklet contains 100 gloss colour chips of British colour standards and also includes useful notes, tables and appendices.

Federal Standards No 595a
A catalogue of 437 colour chips 1" x ½" applicable to USAAF/USN aircraft and equipment. It is available from *Specifications Activity, Printed Materials Supply Division, Building 197, Naval Weapons Plant, Washington DC 20407, USA*. You should write first to confirm postage rates and current price. Otherwise from *American Information Retrieval Services, 22 Roland Gardens, London SW7 3PL*.

United States Camouflage WWII
An American publication containing 20 colour chips. It is available from *Scale Reproductions, 1313 West Abram, Arlington, Texas 76010, USA*.

British Aviation Colours of WW2
Volume 3 in the RAF Museum Series, published by *Arms and Armour Press, 2−6 Hampstead High Street, London NW3 1PR*. Contains 32 colour chips applicable to WW2 RAF aircraft.

O-Nine Gallery
By Thomas Hitchcock published by *Monogram Aviation, Publications Dept 200, 625 Edgebrook Drive, Boylston, Massachusetts 01505, USA*. Contains 32 colour chips of WW2 Luftwaffe aircraft on the last page plus descriptive breakdown of uses.

Methuen Handbook of Colour
By A. Kornerup and Wanscher. Contains chips showing all variations of colour tone along with detailed annotations. Published by *Methuen & Co., Ltd., 11 New Fetter Lane, London EC4*, now out of print, but hopefully to return to circulation.

HUMBROL PAINTS — WW1 AERO COLOUR TABLE

COLOUR NAME		METHUEN REF	HUMBROL MIX	APPLICATION
AUSTRO – HUNGARY WW1				
Prussian Blue	⎫	21F6	15 Midnight Blue	
Dark Maroon	⎪	9F6	3 parts 177 Hull Red + 1 part 33 Black	
Dark Sage	Dark ⎬	29F3	Dark Green 30	Six colour hexagonal camouflage for
Mauve	⎪	15E4	None — N9 Mauve Obsolete	uppersurfaces Aviatik D1 etc.
Ultramarine	⎪	21C5	Matt Blue 25	
Brown Ochre	⎭	6E5	29 Dark Earth	
Light Blue	⎫	25B5	Equal parts 3 Brunswick Green + 64 Light Grey + dash 14 French Blue	
Pale Violet	⎪	14B4	20 Crimson + 22 Gloss White	
Light Green	Light ⎬	28C3	2 parts 80 Grass Green + 1 part 69 Yellow	Six colour hexagonal camouflage for uppersurfaces Aviatik D1 etc.
Ochre	⎪	4B3	62 Leather + dash 7 Light Buff	
Pink Grey	⎪	9B2	64 Light Grey + dash 19 Bright Red	
Blue Grey	⎭	26B3	3 Brunswick Green + 90 Beige Green	
Clear doped Linen		4A3	Obsolete	Undersurfaces
Dark Green		30(E – F)6	30 Dark Green + dash 69 Yellow	⎱ Mottle on upper surfaces. Phonix D1
Dark Earth		5(D – E)4	29 Dark Earth + dash 22 White	⎰ etc.
All finishes are semi-gloss				
GREAT BRITAIN WW1				
Clear doped Linen		4A3	Obsolete	Overall/undersurfaces
PC10		4F(2 – 8)	108 Green + dash 9 Tan	Uppersurface camouflage
PC12		8(E – F)8	113 Rust	Uppersurface camouflage
Nivo		27F3	30 Dark Green + dash 27 Sea Grey	Overall on Night Bombers, 1918 onwards
Light Grey		(B – C)1	64 Light Grey	Plywood panel/cowlings
Vermillion (Roundel Red)		9C8	99 Lemon + dash of 69 Yellow	National Insignia
Ultramarine (Roundel Blue)		20E8	25 Matt Blue	National Insignia
Dull Red (Night Red)		8E8	113 Rust	National Insignia
Dull Blue (Night Blue)		20G4	Obsolete	National Insignia
All finishes are semi-gloss				
FRANCE WW1				
Clear doped Linen		4A3	Obsolete	Early overall/undersurfaces finish
Aluminium		—	3 parts 11 Silver + 2 parts Aircraft Blue 65	Overall/Undersurfaces
Dark Green		30E3	92 Iron Grey + dash 102 Army Green	⎱ Disruptive uppersurfaces camouflage on early
Dark Earth		6E3	70 Brick Red + dash 64 Light Grey	⎰ machines. Used with Aluminium u/surfaces
Light Yellow		4B4	Linen 74 + dash 64 Light Grey	Metal Panels on clear doped a/c
Pale Green		30B3	90 Beige Green	Metal panels on aluminium doped a/c
Silver Grey	(A)	—	11 Silver + 64 Light Grey	Mid overall/undersurfaces finish
Light Yellow	(A)	4C3	HN4 — Obsolete	Mid overall/undersurfaces finish
†Dark Green	(A)	3F3	92 Iron Grey + dash 30 Dark Green	⎫ Disruptive camouflage on uppersurfaces
†Light Green	(A)	3E4	102 Army Green + dash 90 Beige Green	⎪ of late a/c inc. those in Belgian, Italian
†Beige	(A)	5D5	63 Sand + 62 Leather	⎬ and AEF Services.
†Dark Brown	(A)	5E3	10 Service Brown + 98 Chocolate	⎪ Used with Silver Grey or Light Yellow
†Black	(A)	—	21 Black	⎭ undersurfaces
Roundel Red		10D8	19 Bright Red	⎱ National Insignia
Roundel Blue		23D4	48 Mediterranean Blue + dash 40 Pale Grey	⎰

†N.B. (A) These finishes (Humbrol) contain Aluminium (HB14) in sufficient quantity to just begin to show an Aluminium sheen in with the colour.
All finishes are semi-matt

GERMANY WW1

Colour	Code	Mix/Match	Notes
Dark Violet	17F8	68 Purple	Disruptive camouflage on uppersurfaces ie, Albatros DIII/DV
Dark Green	25D8	3 Brunswick Green + dash 14 French Blue	
Pale Blue	23B3	47 Sea Blue + dash 64 Light Grey	Undersurfaces
Dark Brown	6E8	29 Dark Earth + 18 Orange	Disruptive camouflage on uppersurfaces, ie, Fokker DIII, Halberstadt DIII etc.
Dark Green	26F3	91 Black Green	
Mauve	18D6	68 Purple + dash 14 French Blue	
Pale Blue	24B4	65 Aircraft Blue	Undersurfaces
Grey	1(C – D)1	64 Light Grey	Metal panels, cowlings
Bright Green	26D8/E8	2 Emerald + dash 48 Mediterranean Blue	Tail colours: Jasta 5
Rose Red	11B8	19 Bright Red	
Grey Blue	21E7	67 Tank Grey	
Greyish Magenta	14E5	20 Crimson + dash 14 French Blue	Handpainted Hexagonal finish used with black on upper and lower surfaces and used on AEG, Gotha Bombers etc.
Dark Green	26F5	3 Brunswick Green	
Blue	21D4	67 Tank Grey	4 colour painted fabric uppersurfaces Fighters and two-seaters
Turquoise	(24 – 25)E7	3 Brunswick Green + dash 14 French Blue	
Beige	(4 – 5)D4	62 Leather + dash 7 Light Buff	
Green	(29 – 30)D5	78 Cockpit Green	
Pale Blue	23D4	157 Azure Blue	4 colour printed fabric lower surfaces Fighters and two-seaters
Green	26D4	3 Brunswick Green + dash 90 Beige Green	
Ochre	(4 – 5)C7	63 Sand	
Rose	11B5	61 Flesh	
Violet	17E(5 – 6)	68 Purple	5 colour printed fabric uppersurfaces Fighters and two-seaters
Khaki	(4 – 5)D6	62 Leather	
Green	28D(5 – 6)	Obsolete	
Turquoise	24(E – F)6	3 Brunswick Green + dash 14 French Blue	
Blue	21E(6 – 7)	67 Tank Grey	
Magenta	(14 – 15)D4	20 Crimson + dash 14 French Blue	5 colour printed fabric lower surfaces Fighters and two-seaters
Wheat	(4 – 5)B6	Blue	
Ruby	12(C – D)5	62 Leather + dash 7 Light Buff	
Green	(24 – 35)D4	107 Purple	
		3 Brunswick Green + dash 14	
Blue	(21 – 22)D6	French Blue	
		67 Tank Grey	

All finishes are semi-gloss

ITALY WW1

Colour	Code	Mix/Match	Notes
Dark Green	30F7	30 Dark Green + dash 24 Trainer Yellow	Mottle finish on fighters (uppersurfaces)
Light Green	30D6	38 Lime + dash 64 Light Grey	
Sand	4A5	74 Linen	
National Red	11D8	107 Purple	Roundel colours and/or bands on lower wing surfaces.
National Green	28E7	38 Lime + dash 64 Light Grey	
Silver Grey	24C3	175 Hellgrau	Undersurfaces/overall, ie, Nieuport 17 etc.
Silver Grey	—	11 Silver + 64 Light Grey	

All finishes are semi-gloss

HUMBROL PAINTS — WW2 AERO COLOUR TABLE

AUSTRALIA WW2

Colour	Code	Mix/Match	Notes
Foliage Green	3F4	66 Olive Drab	Used overall or as disruptive pattern with Dark Earth
Dark Earth	5(E – F)4	29 Dark Earth	Used as disruptive pattern with Foliage or Dark Green
Dark Green	30(F – G)2	30 Dark Green	Used with Dark Earth as disruptive camouflage pattern
Pale Blue	23A2	47 Sea Blue + dash 34 Matt White	Undersurfaces
(Later Azure Blue)	21B5	157 Azure Blue	
Roundel Blue	20F5	Obsolete	National Insignia

All finishes matt

GREAT BRITAIN WW2

Colour	Code	Mix/Match	Notes
Dark Earth	5(EF)4	29 Dark Earth	Used with Dark Green as disruptive pattern: European

GREAT BRITAIN WW2 Cont'd

Light Earth	5D4	4 parts 29 Dark Earth + 1 part 34 Matt White	Used with Light Green as disruptive pattern on lower wings of biplanes
Dark Green	30(F – G)4	30 Dark Green	Used with Dark Earth as disruptive pattern: European
Light Green	30F4	4 parts 30 Dark Green + 1 part 34 Matt White	Used with Light Earth as disruptive pattern on lower wings of biplanes
Sky	30(B – C)2	90 Beige Green	Used on undersurfaces — European/ Coastal Command FAA etc.
Ocean Grey	24D(2 – 3)	106 Ocean Grey	Used with Dark Green as disruptive pattern with HB6 undersurfaces
Sea Grey Medium	22D3	64 Light Grey	Undersurfaces
Dark Sea Grey	21E3	27 Sea Grey	Used on uppersurfaces, Coastal Command/FAA
Light Slate Grey	26E3	4 parts 92 Iron Grey + 1 part 24 Trainer Yellow	Used on lowersurfaces, Coastal Command/FAA
Mixed Grey	23E3	1 part 27 Sea Grey + spot 34 White + spot 64 Light Grey	Temporarily used until Ocean Grey available
Extra Dark Sea Grey	21F3	HB7	
Dark Slate Grey	29F2	102 Army Green	
Mid Stone	4D7	84 Mid Stone	With Dk Earth as camouflage — Overseas
P.R.U. Mauve	18(E – F)4	2 parts 25 + 3 parts 70 + spot 34	Low level photographic colours
Extra Dark Sea Green	27F4	1 part 116 Green + spot 64 Light Grey	
Dark Sea Green	27(E – F)4	1 part 116 Green + 2 spots 64 Light Grey	Also used in PRU work and on certain Beaufighters in the Bay of Biscay
Sea Green	27E(2 – 3)	92 Iron Grey	
Sky Blue	(23 – 24)A2	1 part 175 Hellgrau + 1 part 34 White	Used on Warwick, Liberator and Fortress over the Atlantic 1944 – 45, with Sky Grey
Deep Sky	21E6	3 parts 25 Blue + 1 part 89 Mid Blue	Partly used in the Middle East
Mediterranean Light Blue	21(D – E)5	1 part 89 Mid Blue + spot 96 RAF Blue	Used as upper colours for Blenheim and Beaufort for maritime work in Middle East. 1942 and on.
Mediterranean Dark Blue	21(E – F)6	3 parts 25 + 1 part 89 + spot 77	
Azure Blue	21B5	157 Azure Blue	Undersurfaces: Overseas
PRU Blue	23E4	106 Ocean Grey	Photo Reconnaissance — overall
Roundel Red, Bright	10C6	60 Matt Scarlet	National Insignia 1930 – 1936
Roundel Blue, Bright	20E8	25 Matt Blue	
Roundel Red, Dull	8D7	113 Rust	National Insignia 1941 – 1946
Roundel Blue, Dull	20F5	Obsolete	
Roundel/Trainer Yellow	(4 – 5)A8	24 Trainer Yellow	Trainers — undersides
Aluminium	—	4 parts 11 Silver + 1 part 64 Light Grey	
Night	—	33 Matt Black	Overall and undersurfaces
Aircraft Grey Green	27D3	78 Cockpit Green	Cockpit Interiors — most a/c
Sky Grey	22C2	166 Lt Aircraft Grey + dash 23 Duck Egg Blue	Used on undersurfaces FAA, 1939 – 1940

All finishes are matt

GERMANY WW2

00 Wasserhell	None	35 Clear Gloss	A clear varnish additive to achieve a gloss finish
02 Silber	None	11 Silver	A top coat and/or primer colour. Used also as a marine anti-fouling finish for floats and hulls
02 RLM Grau	1(D – E)3 to 27(D – E)2	92 Iron Grey or 31 Slate Grey	Early marine camouflage colour; also used as an internal finish and as a general colour on some land-planes, also cockpit areas
03 Silber	None	11 Silver + dash 64 Light Grey	Early overall finish for all types of surface, later replaced by colour 63
04 Gelb	4(A – B)8	10 parts 24 Trainer Yellow + 1 part 60 Scarlet	For identification and fuel grade markings, also used for marine trainers, and 'theatre' and unit markings.
05 Rahm	3B5	74 Matt Linen	Early overall finish for gliders and sail-planes
21 Weiss	None	Matt 34 White	Identification colour/markings, for internal instruments and aircraft systems (ie, fuel, air and hydraulic pipes). Also external for warnings etc. National insignia colours.
22 Schwarz	None	Matt 33 Black	Early night camouflage

GERMANY WW2 Cont'd

23 Rot	(9 – 10)B8	60 Scarlet + dash 34 White	Unit markings, etc.
24 Dunkelblau	21(E – F)6	1 part 104 Oxford Blue + 1 part 109 Blue + 5 parts 34 White	Limited overall colour for pre-war machines, sometimes with 23 Rot
25 Hellgrun	26D(7 – 8)	1 part 109 Blue + 1 part 101 Mid Green	Staff aircraft identification colour
26 Braun	(7 – 8)(E – 8)	Obsolete	
27 Gelb	3(B – C)(7 – 8)	24 Trainer Yellow + dash of 33 Black	Mostly used for 'theatre' markings
28 Weinrot	(10 – 11)F8	5 parts 98 Chocolate + 2 parts 60 Scarlet	Used for marking walkway areas and trim tabs
41 Mittelgrau	22D2	64 Light Grey + dash 33 Black	Internal finish also a primer colour. A lighter grey 1(B – C)1 used for instrument panels up to 1942
61 Dunkelbraun	8(E – F)6	HM21 — Obsolete	Camouflage colour used mostly on bombers with 62 and 63.
62 Grun	27(E – F)5	5 parts 76 Uniform Green + 1 part 80 Grass Green	Camouflage colour used mostly on bombers with 61 and 63
63 Hellgrau	(1 – 2)(B – C)2	1 part 64 Light Grey + 97 Eggshell	Overall aircraft colour in place of 03 also camouflage colour used on bombers with 61 and 62
65 Hellblau	24(B – C)4	5 parts 175 Hellgrau + 2 parts 109 Blue + 5 parts 34 White	Undersurface camouflage colour used throughout WWII
66 Schwarzgrau	21F(1 – 2)	67 Tank Grey + dash 64 Light Grey	Camouflage colour. Interior of cockpits armour plate colour
70 Schwarzgrun	28G2	HG15 — obsolete	Basic landplane camouflage colour usually used with 71. Also used for prop blades when mixed with 00
71 Dunkelgrun	(29 – 30)F3	30 Dark Green + dash 102 Army Green	Basic landplane camouflage colour usually used with 70
72 Grun	26F3	5 parts 67 Tank Grey + 2 parts 101 Mid Green	Basic camouflage colour on seaplanes or landplanes operating over water. Used singly or with 73
73 Grun	26G3	4 parts 30 Dark Green + 1 part 67 Tank Grey	Basic camouflage colour on seaplanes or landplanes operating over water. Usually used with 72
74 Dunkelgrau	26F2	1 part 91 Black Green + 1 part 92 Iron Grey	Camouflage colour often used with 75 & 76. Only for fighters, night fighters and Zerstorer aircraft
75 Mittelgrau	22E2	79 Blue Grey + 1 part 34 White	Camouflage colour often used with 74 & 76. Same applications as 74.
76 Hellgrau (Weissblau)	(23 – 24)A2	23 Duck Egg Blue + dash 22 White	
77 Hellgrau (Graulich)	30B(1 – 2)	8 parts 22 White + 1 part 21 Black	Only for lettering and national insignia in night operations, on colour 22
78 Himmelblau	23B(4 – 5)	1 part 109 Blue + 1 part 34 White + dash 64 Light Grey	Undersurface colour for use with desert colours 79 & 80
79 Sandgelb (Temp.)	(4 – 5)C7	63 Sand + dash 24 Trainer Yellow	Early desert camouflage colour
79 Sandbraun	6(D – E)5	62 Leather + dash 70 Brick Red	Uppersurface colour. Used with 78 & 80
80 Olivegrun	(29 – 30)F3	108 Green + dash 29 Dark Earth	Uppersurface colour. Used only over 79
(80?) Mittelbraun (Temp.)	5(E – F)4	29 Dark Earth	Used over 79 Sandgelb and on FW190's during 1943, with 71
81 Braunviolet	3(F – H)2	1 part 66 Olive Green + 1 part 98 Chocolate	Late war upper surface camouflage colour. Used singly or with 82 or 83. Undersurface colour 76
82 Dunkelgrun	(25 – 26)F4	2 parts 88 Deck Green + 1 part 30 Dark Green	Later was uppersurface camouflage colour used with colour 81 or 83 Undersurface colour 76
83 Grun	28E(6 – 7)	HF2 Obsolete	Very late war colour. Used singly or with 81 or 82. Undersurfaces 76
99 Gelb/Grun	1B6	Use a tint of 82 Pale Yellow	Primer enamel and anodic finish. Often used on cowling fasteners and other internal components having no special colour importance

*All finishes semi-gloss

FRANCE WW2

Kaki	4E7	1 part 26 Khaki + spot 34 White + 64 Light Grey	Uppersurface disruptive pattern, used with Vert, Terre Fonce, Gris Bleu Fonce
Vert	27E5	H.F.2. Obsolete	Used with above. Overall colour on certain a/c and cockpit interiors

FRANCE WW2 Cont'd

Terre Fonce	6(E – F)7	H.F.3. Obsolete	Uppersurface disruptive pattern, see above
Gris Bleu Clair	23A4	1 part 89 Middle Blue + 1 part 34 White	Undersurfaces
Gris Bleu Fonce	22D3	79 Blue Grey	Uppersurface disruptive pattern. See above. Also used as basic finish on Vichy a/c
Chocolate (gloss)	6F4 (Approx)	98 Chocolate + spot 70 Brick Red	Pre-1939 Bombers — overall or sometimes with Black undersurfaces
Vert (gloss)	27(E – F)8	H.F.2. Obsolete	Pre-1939 Fighters — overall
Gris foncee	23D2	64 Light Grey	
Gris bleu foncee	21E3	176 Neutral Grey	
Gris vert foncee	28D(4 – 5)	1 part 80 Grass Green + 1 part 34 White	Maritime — uppersurfaces
Gris bleu	21(C – D)3	106 Ocean Grey	
Gris bleu clair	22B2	1 part 34 White + spot 157 Azure Blue	Later maritime undersurfaces
Argent	—	4 parts 11 Silver + 1 part 64 Light Grey	Early overall finish all types
Gris vert clair	29C3	1 part 102 Army Green + spot 34 White	Internal airframe finish
Night Blue	None	Obsolete	Cockpit interiors
Roundel Blue	23D4	48 Mediterranean Blue + dash 40 Pale Grey	National Insignia
Roundel Red	10D8	19 Bright Red	
Vichy Yellow	3A8	24 Trainer Yellow	Used up to 1942 with red as stripes on nose and tail

ITALY WW2

Alluminio (Aluminium) + *	—	1 part Silver 11 + spot 64 Light Grey	Early overall and undersurface finish
Grigio Azzurro Chiaro (Lt Grey)—□ ● 1	28D2	1 part 64 Light Grey + spot 102 Army Green	Later undersurface colour; naval included
Grigio Mimetico (Medium Grey)	23(D – E)2	H.J.4. Obsolete	
Grigio Azzurro Scuro 3 (Dark Grey) 1	23F2	1 part 27 Sea Grey + spot 33 Black	Uppersurfaces naval a/c (Scheme includes all 1)
Bianco Avorio 5 (Buff)	(4 – 5)B3	1 part 34 White + spot 94 Brown Yellow + spot 63 Sand	Early 3 colour camouflage for Spain etc. (includes +)
Giallo Mimetico 1 (Cream) +	4B5	1 part 74 Linen + spot 34 White + spot 63 Sand	
Giallo Mimetico 2 (Light Sand)	4C6	2 parts 74 Linen + 1 part 81 Pale Yellow	Early 3 colour camouflage, home and overseas (includes *)
Giallo Mimetico 3 (Golden Sand)*	(4 – 5)C7	1 part 94 Brown Yellow + spot 84 Mid Stone + 76 Uniform Green	
Giallo Mimetico 4 (Dark Sand) —	(4 – 5)D5	1 part 94 Brown Yellow + 84 Mid Stone + spot Uniform Green + spot 110 Natural Wood	
Bruno Mimetico (Light Tan)	5E4	1 part 118 Tan + spot 29 Dark Earth	Overseas colouring (includes □)
Nicciola Chiaro 4 (Mid Tan) □	5E5	1 part 29 Dark Earth + spot 24 + spot 160	
Marrone Mimetico 1 (Light Brown)	6(D – E)5	1 part 110 Natural Wood + spot 29 Dark Earth	
" " 53193 (Dk Brown) +	7F5	1 part 29 Dark Earth + spot 60 + spot 24	
" " 2 (Red Brown) *	8E8	1 part 160 + spot 60 + spot 98	
Verde Mimetico 1 (Lt Olive Green) + *	2E6	1 part 11 + spot 24	
Verde Mimetico 53192 (Med Green)	28E5	1 part 80 + spot 86	
Verde Mimetico 2 (Blue Green)	27F5	Obsolete	Western desert variation (includes—)
Verde Mimetico 3 (Olive Green)	30F3	1 part 30 + spot 24	Standard home uppersurface colour
Verde Oliva Scuro 2 (Dark Green)□ ●	27F3	Obsolete	(includes ●) Interior finish
Verde anticorosione (Light Grey-Green primer)	27B3	1 part 90 + spot 65	Ident. colour and National markings
Bianco Neve 6 (White)	—	34 White	Ident. colour
Giallo Cromo 7 (Deep Yellow)	5A8	1 part 24 + spot 60	Ident. colour and National markings
Rosso 8 (Red)	10D8	1 part 60 + spot 73	Ident. colour and National markings
Verde 9 (Green)	27(E – F)8	101 Mid Green	Ident. colour
Bruno Rossiccio 10 (Red Brown)	9(E – F)7	70 Brick Red	Ident. colour
Azzurro 11 (Ultramarine)	21D8	25 Blue	Ident. colour
Nero 12 (Black)	—	33 Black	

*All colours matt (Symbols — □ ● 1 + * refer to all colours belonging to a scheme)*

RUSSIA WW2

Dull aluminium	C1	1 part 11/68 + 65	Early overall finish
Light Grey	3C2	162 Surface Grey	Subsequent overall finish, and undersurface finish with camouflage
Very Light Grey	3B2	1 part 162 + spot 34 White	Undersurface and ident. colour
Brownish-Green	27(E – F)6	1 part 114 + spot 29 Dark Earth	Early upper surface colour. Overall on some bombers
Dark Olive-Green	29F3	1 part 114 + spot 118 Tan	Later uppersurface colour with Dark Brown
Dark Brown	5(E – F)5	118 Tan	Camouflage with Dark Olive-Green

All finishes matt or semi-matt — Literal English translation of colour names has been made

RUSSIA WW2 Cont.

Dark Grey	24(D – E)2	1 part Light Grey 64 + spot 33 Black	Naval finish and with Dark Olive-Green, in place of Dark Brown
Pale Blue-Grey	24(C – D)3	115 Russian Blue	Later undersurface colour
Ident Red	9(C – D)8	Obsolete	National Markings
Ident Yellow	3A8 ·	99 Lemon	For stencilled instructions etc.
Interior Grey Green	27(C – D)2	1 part 78 + spot 34 White	Internal finish
White	—	34 White	Indent. colour
Black	—	33 Black	Indent. colour, and night camouflage

JAPAN WW2

Dark Green N1*	25F3	H.J.1. — Obsolete	Uppersurfaces — navy a/c
Very Pale Grey A/N2	B1	H.J.2. — Obsolete	Undersurfaces — army/navy a/c
Dark Grey Green A3	29(E – F)3	H.J.3. — Obsolete	U/surfaces — army a/c & for camouflage
Medium chrome Yellow A/N4	3A(5 – 6)	1 part 24 + spot 74	Overall trainer colour
Sky Grey A5	23A2	1 part 64 + spot 34	Early overall finish army a/c
Dull Aluminium A6	C1	1 part 11 Silver + spot 65	Overall finish — army a/c
Sea Grey A7	23D(2 – 3)	64 Light Grey	Overall finish as on Nate, Mary and Nick
Pale Blue-Grey N8	24(B – C)2	1 part 175 Hellgrau + spot 34	Undersurfaces some navy a/c
Pale Grey-Violet N9	17D3	H.J.4. — Obsolete	Overall float plane finish
Very Pale Blue-Grey N10	23A(2 – 3)	1 part 34 White + spot 65	Overall finish — navy a/c
Medium Blue N11	21(D – E)4	1 part 96 RAF Blue + spot 34 White	Uppersurface finish as on Frank
Blue-Grey N12	24C(4 – 5)	1 part 89 + spot 34	Undersurface finish — navy a/c
Pale Yellow N13	2A7	74 Linen	Early overall finish — navy a/c
Dark Indian Red A/N14	8(E – F)7	70 Brick Red	Often used as a propeller finish
Light Khaki N15	3C7	1 part Pale Yellow 81 + spot 83	Camouflage with N1, as on Betty
Crimson A/N16	10D8	1 part 60 Scarlet + spot 73	Ident. colour
Light Brown N17	5E5	110 Natural Wood	Army a/c with N1 on upper surfaces
Pale Geranium A/N18	8C8	1 part 60 Scarlet + spot 24	Insignia Red (Hinomaru)
Maroon N19	10F5	1 part 73 + spot 77	Used as a metal primer under camouflage
Deep Yellow A/N20	4A(7 – 8)	1 part 24 + spot 60	Ident. colour
Bright Blue A/N21	20(C – D)8	1 part 25 + spot 89	Ident. colour
Black A/N22	—	33 Black	Ident. colour
White A/N23	—	34 White	Ident. colour
Pale Olive-Grey A/N24	30B3	95 concrete	Undersurfaces 1945 — as on Peggy
Sienna A/N25	6D7	1 part 62 + spot 10	Uppersurfaces — as on Tojo
Dark Blue-Grey N26	23F2	77 Navy Blue	Later uppersurface colour, as on Peggy
Light Olive-Green A27	1F6	1 part 102 + spot 80	Later uppersurface colour — army a/c
Interior Green/Blue A/N28	—	52 Baltic Blue	Internal finish, wheel wells etc.

Colour names are a visual description of actual colours. Hues numbered for reference with 'A' prefix for Army use and 'N' for Navy use.

UNITED STATES OF AMERICA WW2

Olive Drab 41 ANA 613	4F7	66 Olive Drab + spot 102	Uppersurfaces — 1941 onwards
Medium Green 42 ANA 612	28F6	Obsolete	U/surfaces fighters in Europe from 1943 (used as patches over OD41 on bombers)
Interior Green ANA 611	30F8	158 Interior Green	Interior cockpit 1941 onwards
Middlestone ANA 615	4(D – E)4	84 Mid Stone	
Sand 49 ANA 616 (Desert pink)	(6 – 7)C3	1 part 29 Dark Earth + 3 parts 34 + spot 60	Early desert camouflage with OD41
Desert Drab ANA 628	6(D – E)4	1 part 29 + 2 parts 34	Later desert uppersurface finish
Dark Earth ANA 617	5(E – F)4	29 Dark Earth	
Neutral Grey 43	24E2 (Approx)	176 Neutral Grey	Undersurfaces: On some a/c replaced by Light Gray after 1943
Light Gray ANA 602	22C2 (Approx)	64 Light Grey	1939 – 41. Overall. Then undersurfaces until 1943
Blue Gray ANA 603	22F3(Approx)	176 Neutral Grey + dash 34 White	Uppersurfaces USN — October 1941
Dark Gull Gray ANA 621	2(D – E)3 (Approx)	Obsolete	Mainly used by USN in North Atlantic 1941 – 1945
Light Gull Gray ANA 620	22(B – C)2 (Approx)	3 parts 64 Light Grey + 1 part 34 Matt White	
Aircraft Gray (gloss) ANA 512	24C2(Approx)	64 Light Grey Matt	
Engine Gray (gloss) ANA 513	20F2	Equal parts 5 Dark Grey + 21 Black	Engine crankcases
Non Specular Sea Blue ANA 607	22F4	Obsolete	Uppersurface US Navy—Jan. 1943 onwards
Intermediate Blue ANA 608	22D4(Approx)	96 RAF Blue	USN 1943/44 Fins/Rudder sides of fuselage used with Semi Gloss Sea Blue and White† Undersurface — desert areas
Azure Blue ANA 609	21B5	157 Azure Blue + 34 Matt White	

UNITED STATES OF AMERICA WW2 Cont'd

Semi Gloss Sea Blue ANA 606	22G4(Approx)	30 Dark Green + 49 Matt Varnish	Overall USN finish — March 1944
Glossy Sea Blue ANA 623	22G4(Approx) 28B3	Obsolete	Undersurfaces
Sky Blue ANA 610	21H8(Approx)	90 Beige Green	National Insignia
Insignia Blue 47 ANA 605	10D8	Obsolete	National Insignia
Insignia Red 45 ANA 618	9A8	19 Bright Red	For markings and warnings
Bright Red ANA 619	4A8	60 Scarlet	Idents., also upper surfaces of wings
Ident. Yellow 48 ANA 614	7B8	Obsolete	USN, to 1941
International Orange ANA 508	2(B – C)6 (Approx)	18 Orange	Idents.
Zinc Chromate (Yellow)		81 Pale Yellow	Pre-1941 interiors of cockpit, wheel
Zinc Chromate (Green)	1D6(Approx)	80 Grass Green + spot 99	wells etc.
(Dirty) White	—	3 parts 34 White + spot 64 + spot 24 Trainer Yellow	Dulled by units to a Grey
PBY Gray ANA 625	22F2	2 parts 27 + 2 parts 30 + 2 spots 34 White	USN Patrol colouring
PBY Blue	24F5	2 parts 76 + 1 part 77 + spot 24	Limited use by USN Used by RCAF
PBY Green	25(E – F)5	3 parts 76 + 1 part 77 + spot 24	Atlantic patrols
Strata Blue ANA 516	21G4	2 parts 77 + 1 part 76 + spot 33	USN anti-dazzle, and early 1941 colour
Light Yellow ANA 505	3A8	1 part 99 + spot 34	With Bright Red, formed in 1941 section
Light Blue ANA 501	21D8	1 part 25 + spot 89	and carrier colours USN
Light Green ANA 503	28D8	101 Mid Green	

*All finishes matt unless otherwise stated

ISRAEL CONTEMPORARY

Green 34227	28E6	Obsolete	Disruptive camouflage on uppersurfaces
Earth 30219	6(D – E)4	29 Dark Earth + dash 34 White	
Middlestone 33531	4B2	63 Sand + 34 Matt White	
Pale Blue 35622	24A3	65 Aircraft Blue + 34 White	Lower surfaces
Blue	23F3	67 Tank Grey	Standard tank and vehicle camouflage
Grey	5(C – D)3	Approx equal parts 72 Khaki Drill and Matt White 34	

*All finishes semi-matt

RUSSIA CONTEMPORARY

Ident. Red	10B8	HT5 — Obsolete	National markings
Ident. Blue, bright	22B6	109 Blue	Fighter individual aircraft numerals
Di-electric Green	28E7	80 Grass Green	Early radar panels on fins, nose cones, etc.
Radome Grey	21C3	1 part 64 + spot 96	Later radar panels and nose cones
Dark Buff	5B4	1 part 63 + spot 34	Canopy frame sealing compound
Dark Green	28(F – G)5	1 part 91 + spot 80	
Tan	6(D – E)5	1 part 62 + spot 63	Upper surface camouflage
Stone	(4 – 5)B3	1 part 71 + spot 63	
Very Pale Blue	24A2	1 part 23 + spot 89	Under surface colouring
Ident. Yellow	4A8	24 Trainer Yellow	Stencilled instructions
Ident. Blue, Dull	22D8	25 Blue	Stencilled instructions

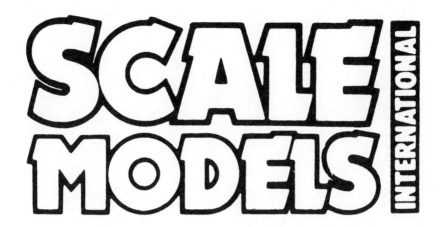
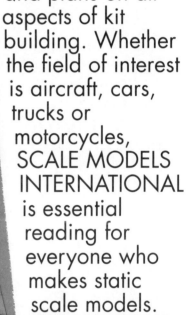